English Prose Fiction, 1600-1700

A Chronological Checklist

COMPILED BY

CHARLES C. MISH

UNIVERSITY OF MARYLAND

BIBLIOGRAPHICAL SOCIETY OF THE UNIVERSITY OF VIRGINIA

CHARLOTTESVILLE, VIRGINIA, 1967

Preface

The present checklist, like its mimeographed predecessor of 1952, is basically a chronological rearrangement of the seventeenth-century material in Arundell Esdaile's *List of English Tales and Prose Romances Printed Before 1740* (London, 1912). There are, of course, some changes. A very few titles in Esdaile have been dropped on the ground that they cannot reasonably be called fiction, a number of titles have been added, and further editions of titles in Esdaile have been included. The 1952 edition of this checklist gives a detailed list of these several changes; rather than repeat this somewhat lengthy and possibly useless list I simply refer the student to that edition.

The form and arrangement of information in the various items in this checklist should be largely self-explanatory. Each item is assigned to a year (some arbitrarily, of necessity), under which it is entered by its author's name, or, in the case of anonymous titles, by catchword. Titles have generally been shortened; imprints omit addresses. Following the imprint a note in curves identifies the item by giving its entry number in Pollard and Redgrave or Wing; this reference will serve both as an independent confirmation of the item and as a location device. When an item is not to be found in either of the two Short-Title Catalogues, I have given instead of the entry number the source of my information; in a few cases this will take the form of a reference to a bookseller's catalogue (e.g. Muirhead, Quaritch). Finally comes a statement of edition, though if there is only one edition of a given title, no comment is made.

It may be pointed out also that the dates to which undated editions are assigned frequently do not agree with those given in Wing for the items in question. I have attempted to place each such undated edition in a year consonant with the working period of its printer or publisher, though this has meant at times merely putting the book in the mid-point of a sweep of years in a rather mechanical way. This forced dating results in dumping a number of titles in convenient round-number years like 1675, 1680, 1690, and, especially, 1700; in this last year all the dubious productions hovering around the turn of the century are given a place, even though some of them undoubtedly could be moved out because they are post-seventeenth-century titles. Assigned dates are shown in square brackets.

Charles C. Mish

College Park, Md.

ENGLISH PROSE FICTION, 1600-1700

1600

ALBIONS QUEEN. The famous history of Albions queene. W. White, for T. Pavier. —Dedication signed R. G. (STC 11502)

ARMIN, ROBERT. Foole upon foole, or Six sortes of sottes. [By] Clonnico de Curtanio Snuffe. For W. Ferbrand. (Folger Library. First edition; reprinted 1605; re-issued with additions, 1608, as *A nest of ninnies.*)

BRETON, NICHOLAS. The strange fortunes of two excellent princes. P. Short, for N. Ling. (STC 3702)

CHAMBERS, ROBERT. Palestina written by Mr. R. C. P. and Bachelor of Divinitie. Florence [i.e. London?]: B. Sermartelli [i.e. J. Wolfe?]. (STC 4954)

GESTA ROMANORUM. A record of auncient histories, intituled in Latin: Gesta Romanorum. The sixth impression. T. East. (Esdaile; Boston Public Library. Sixth edition of Robinson's version, which first appeared ca.1577; two earlier undated editions exist, and one dated 1557.)

GREENE, ROBERT. Greenes Groatsworth of wit. (Cited by Esdaile, without imprint, from the *Censura Literaria.* Third edition; earlier editions in 1592, 1596.)

GREENE, ROBERT. Greenes Never too late. J. Roberts for N. Ling. (STC 12254. Second edition; first edition in 1590.)

KITTOWE, ROBERT. Loves loadstarre. T. Creede. (STC 15026)

OCEANDER. The heroicall adventures of the Knight of the Sea . . .

Prince Oceander. For W. Leake. (STC 18763)

ROBERTS, HENRY. Haigh for Devonshire. T. Creede. (STC 21081. First edition.)

1601

ALBIONS QUEEN. [The famous historie of Albions Queene.] W. W. for T. Pavier. (Esdaile)

BIDPAI. The morall philosophie of Doni: drawne out of the ancient writers. Englished by Sir Thomas North. S. Stafford. (STC 3054. Second edition; first edition in 1570.)

GREENE, ROBERT. Ciceronis amor. For N. Lynge. (STC 12226. Fourth edition; earlier editions in 1589, 1592, 1597.)

GREENE, ROBERT. Penelopes web. For J. Hodgets. (STC 12294. Second edition; first edition in 1587.)

HUON OF BORDEAUX. The ancient, honorable, famous, and delightful historie of Huon of Bourdeaux. Being the third time imprinted. T. Purfoot, sould by E. White. (STC 13999. Third edition; first edition ca.1534, second edition lost. Translated by Lord Berners.)

LYLY, JOHN. Euphues and his England. J. R. for G. Cawood. (STC 17076. Eleventh edition; earlier editions in 1580 (ter), 1581, 1582, 1584, 1586, 1588, 1592, 1597.)

ORTUÑEZ DE CALAHORRA, DIEGO. The ninth part of the Mirrour of knighthood. For C. Burbie. (STC 18871)

1602

AESOP. The etymologist of Aesops Fables. Compiled by Simon Sturtevant. R. Field for R. Dexter. (STC 23410. Only edition of this version, an interlinear literal translation for students.)

CORROZET, G I L L E S. Memorable conceits of divers noble and famous personages of Christendome. For J. Shaw. (STC 5795)

GESTA ROMANORUM. A record of auncient histories, intituled in Latin: Gesta Romanorum. The seventh impression. T. East. (Esdaile. Seventh edition of this version.)

GREENE, ROBERT. Greenes Never too late. For N. Ling. (Folger Library. Third edition.)

PALMERIN OF ENGLAND. The third and last part of Palmerin of England. Translated by A[nthony] M[unday]. J. R. for W. Leake. (STC 19165)

SEVEN SAGES. The hystorie of the seven wise maisters of Rome, newlye corrected. T. Purfoote. (Huntington Library. Fourth edition; earlier editions dated [1493], [1520?], [1555?].)

1603

DEKKER, THOMAS. 1603. The wonderfull yeare. T. Creede. (STC 6534. First of three editions; cf. next entry and entry for 1604.)

DEKKER, THOMAS. The wonderfull yeare. 1603. T. Creede. (STC 6535. Second edition, undated; subsequent to preceding entry, but may be as late as 1604.)

PEEBLES. The thrie tailes of the thrie priests of Peblis . . . supplyit with sundrie merie tailes. Edinburgh: R.

Charteris. (STC 19528. The marginal merry tales are selected from *A C. mery tales.*)

1604

B R E T O N, NICHOLAS. Grimellos fortunes. For E. White. (STC 3657)

DEKKER, THOMAS. The wonderfull yeare. 1603. T. Creede. (Third edition, undated; subsequent to previous two editions, but may be as late as 1607.)

HIND, JOHN. The most excellent historie of Lysimachus and Varrona. By J. H. R. T. Creede. (STC 13510)

JACK OF DOVER. Jacke of Dover, his quest of inquirie. For W. Ferbrand. (STC 14291. First edition.)

LODGE, THOMAS. Rosalynde, Euphues golden legacie. J. R. for N. Lyng. (STC 16668. Fifth edition; earlier editions in 1590, 1592, 1596, 1598.)

LODGE, THOMAS. Rosalynde, Euphues golden legacie. For J. Smethwick. (STC 16668a. Sixth edition.)

PASQUIL. Pasquils jests, mixed with Mother Bunches merriments. For J. Browne. (STC 19451. First edition.)

1605

ARMIN, ROBERT. Foole upon foole, or, Six sortes of sottes. [By] Clonnico del mondo Snuffe. For W. Ferbrand. (Folger Library. Second edition.)

EVORDANUS. The first and second part of the History of the famous Evordanus Prince of Denmark. J. R. for R. B. (John Rylands Library)

GREENE, ROBERT. Ciceronis amor. J. R. for N. Lyng. (STC 12227. Fifth edition.)

6

GREENE, ROBERT. M e n a p h o n. (Cited by Esdaile, without imprint, from the *Censura Literaria*. Third edition; earlier editions in 1589, 1599.)

HELIODORUS. An Aethiopian historie. For W. Cotton. (STC 13044. Fourth edition; earlier editions appeared in [1569?], 1577, 1587. Translated by Thomas Underdowne.)

LYLY, JOHN. Euphues. The anatomie of wit. For W. Leake. (Esdaile. Thirteenth edition; earlier editions dated [1578], [1579], 1579, 1580, 1581, 1582, 1585, 1587, [1590?], [1592], [1595?], [1597?].)

LYLY, JOHN. Euphues and his England. For W .Leake. (STC 17077. Twelfth edition.)

SIDNEY, Sir PHILIP. The Countesse of Pembrokes Arcadia. Now the fourth time published. For S. Waterson. (STC 22543, Fifth edition; earlier editions in 1590 (2 issues), 1593, 1598, 1599. —Another issue of the present edition appeared also in 1605, with imprint: For M. Lownes [STC 22543a].)

URANO. [The most famous and delightfull history of Urano otherwise called the Grene knighte.] (Esdaile. Lost.)

1606

BRETON, NICHOLAS. The miseries of Mavillia. (In: The wil of wit. T. Creede. STC 3703. Third edition; earlier editions in 1597, 1599.)

DEKKER, THOMAS. Newes from Hall. R. B. for W. Ferebrand. (STC 6514. Revised as *A knights conjuring*, 1607.)

FLORES, JUAN DE. A paire of turtle doves, or, The tragicall history of Bellora and Fidelio. For F. Burton. (STC 11094. Another version appeared in 1608.)

HELIODORUS. An Aethiopian historie. For W. Cotton. (STC 13045. Fifth edition. Translated by Thomas Underdowne.)

HIND, JOHN. Eliosto Libidinoso. V. Simmes, sold by N. Butter. (STC 13509)

LYLY, JOHN. Euphues. The anatomie of wit. For W. Leake. (STC 17061. Fourteenth edition.)

LYLY, JOHN. Euphues and his England. For W. Leake. (STC 17078. Thirteenth edition.)

MORE, Sir THOMAS. A frutefull, pleasant, & wittie worke, of the best state of a publique weale, and of the new ile called Utopia. A. Vcale. (Esdaile. Fourth edition of the English translation by Robinson; earlier editions in 1551, 1556, 1597.)

RICH, BARNABY. Rich his farewell to militarie profession. G. E. for T. Adams. (STC 20997. Fourth edition; earlier editions in 1581, 1583, 1594.)

1607

APOLLONIUS. The patterne of painfull adventures. Translated into English by L. Twine Gent. V. Sims. (STC 710. First appearance of this version was [1594?].)

CARTIGNY, JEAN DE. The voyage of the wandering knight. Translated by W[illiam] G[oodyear]. T. Este. (STC 4701. Second edition; first edition in 1581.)

DEKKER, THOMAS. A knights conjuring. T. C. for W. Barley. (STC

7

6508. First appeared in 1606 as *Newes from Hell*.)

DEKKER, THOMAS, and WILKINS GEORGE. Jests to make you merie. N. O. for N. Butter. (STC 6541)

DOBSON, George. Dobsons drie bobbes: sonne and heire to Skoggin. V. Simmes. (STC 6930)

ESTIENNE, HENRI. A world of wonders. For J. Norton. (STC 10553. First edition.)

FORDE, EMANUEL. The most pleasaunt historie of Ornatus and Artesia. For T. Creede. (STC 11169. Second edition; first edition in [1595?].)

GOULART, SIMON. Admirable and memorable histories containing the wonders of our time. [Translated] by Ed. Grimeston. G. Eld. (STC 12135)

GREENE, ROBERT. Greenes Never too late. For N. Ling. (STC 12255. Fourth edition.)

GREENE, ROBERT. Pandosto, the triumph of time. For G. Potter. (STC 12288. Fourth edition; earlier editions in 1588, 1592, 1595.)

GRISELDA. The antient, true, and admirable history of Patient Grissel. Written in French, and now translated into English. E. All-de. (Esdaile. First edition.)

JOHNSON, RICHARD. The pleasant conceites of Old Hobson the merry Londoner. For J. Wright. (STC 14688. First edition.)

LEFEVRE, RAOUL. The ancient historie of the destruction of Troy. Translated by W. Caxton. Newly corrected by William Fiston. T. Creede. (STC 15380. Sixth edition; earlier editions in [1475?], 1502, 1503. 1553, 1596.)

LYLY, JOHN. Euphues. The anatomie of wit. For W. Leake. (STC 17062. Fifteenth edition.)

MARKHAM, GERVASE. The English Arcadia, alluding his beginning from Sir Philip Sydneys ending. E. Allde, solde by H. Rocket. (STC 17351. Part 2 appeared in 1613.)

PEELE, GEORGE. The merrie conceited jests of George Peele. N. Okes, for F. Faulkner and H. Bell. (STC 19541. First edition.)

1608

ARMIN, ROBERT. A nest of minnies. By Robert Armin. T. E. for J. Deane. (STC 775. Earlier editions appeared in 1600 and 1605 as *Foole upon foole*.)

BELLEFOREST, FRANÇOIS DE. The hystorie of Hamblet. R. Bradocke, for T. Pavier. (Esdaile)

BETTIE, W. The historie of Titana and Theseus. T. C. for T. Pavier. (STC 1980. First edition.)

COBBLER OF CANTERBURY. The cobler of Caunterburie. For N. Butter. (STC 4580. Second edition; first edition in 1590.)

ESTIENNE, HENRI. A world of wonders. Edenburgh: A. Hart and R. Lawson. (STC 10554. Second edition. —Some copies have variant imprint: Edenburgh: A. Hart and R. Lawson for J. Norton.)

FAUST. The historie of the damnable life and deserved death of Doctor John Faustus. J. Windet for E. White. (STC 10712. Second edition; first edition in 1592.)

FLORES, JUAN DE. Histoire de Aurelio, et Isabelle. The historie of Aurelio and of Isabell, nyeuley transslatede in foure langagies, Frenche, Italien, Spanishe, and Inglishe. Bruxelle: J. Mommart, & J. Reyns. (STC 11093. Fourth edition; earlier editions in 1556 (2 issues), 1586, 1588. —Some copies have variant imprint: Bruxelle: J. Mommart.)

FORDE, EMANUEL. The first part of Parismus the renownced Prince of Bohemia. T. Creede. (STC 11172, pt. 1. Second edition; first edition appeared in 1598. —Part 2 of this present edition appeared in 1609.)

GREENE, ROBERT. Greenes Carde of fancie. H. L. for M. Lownes. (STC 12264. Fourth edition; earlier editions as *Gwydonius* in 1584, 1587, 1593.)

JACK OF OF DOVER. Jack of Dover. His quest of inquirie. (Cited by Esdaile, without imprint. Second edition.)

JOHNSON, RICHARD. The most famous history of the seven champions of Christendome. For E. Burbie. (STC 14679. Second edition; first edition in two parts, 1596-97.)

PETTIE, GEORGE. A petite pallace of Pettie his pleasure. G. Eld. (STC 19822. Sixth edition; earlier editions dated [1576], [n.d.], [1578?], [1580?], 1598.)

SAN PEDRO, DIEGO DE. A historie called Arnalt and Lucenda. (In: Desainliens, Claude. *The Italian schoolemaister.* T. Purfoot. STC 6760. Third edition; earlier editions in 1575, 1597.)

WILKINS, GEORGE. The painfull adventures of Pericles Prince of Tyre. T. P. for N. Butter. (STC 19628)

1609

CARTIGNY, JEAN DE. The voyage of the wandering knight. Translated by W[illiam] G[oodyear]. T. Snodham. [1609?] (STC 4702. Third edition.)

FORDE, EMANUEL. Parismenos, the second part of Parismus. T. Creede. STC 11172, pt. 2. Second edition; first edition in 1599. —Part 1 of this present edition appeared in 1608.)

GREENE, ROBERT. Ciceronis amor. For J. Smethwick. (STC 12228. Sixth edition.)

GREENE, ROBERT. Pandosto, the triumph of time. W. Stansby, for G. Potter. (Esdaile; Folger Library. Fifth edition. —Running title: The history of Dorastus and Fawnia.)

HALL, JOSEPH. The discovery of a new world. By an English Mercury. For E. Blount, and W. Barrett. [1609?] STC 12686. First edition. Translated by John Healey from the Latin.)

LODGE, THOMAS. Rosalynd. Euphues golden legacie. For J. Smethwick. (STC 16669. Seventh edition.)

LYLY, JOHN. Euphues and his England. For W. Leake. (STC 17079. Fourteenth edition.)

MORINDOS. The famous & renowned history of Morindos a king of Spaine. For H. R. (STC 18108)

PALMERIN OF ENGLAND. The first part of the . . . historie, of the famous and fortunate prince, Palmerin of England. Translated by A[nthony] M[unday]. T. Creede. (STC 19162. Second edition; first edition in 1596.)

PASQUIL. Pasquils jestes, mixed with Mother Bunches merriments. Whereunto is added a bakers doozen of gulles. For J. Browne. (Folger Library. Second edition.)

9

GESTA ROMANORUM. A record of ancient histories, entituled in Latin: Gesta Romanorum. T. Snodham. (STC 21289. Eighth edition of this version. —Also occurs without the date on the title-page; ninth edition.)

GREENE, ROBERT. Greenes Arcadia, or Menaphon. For J. Smethwick. (STC 12274. Fourth edition.)

JOHNSON, RICHARD. The pleasant conceites of Old Hobson the merry Londoner. For J. Wright. (STC 14689. Second edition.)

MONTREUX, NICOLAS DE. Honours academie. Or the famous pastorall, of the faire shepheardesse, Julietta. Done into English by R[obert] T[ofte]. T. Creede. (STC 18053)

AESOP. Aesop, Avicen [sic?], Alphonce and Poge's Fables. (Cited by Esdaile, without imprint, from the Heber catalogue. Presumably Caxton's version. The thirteenth of eighteen editions of the fables in English during the period up to 1640.)

AESOP. [Fables.] (Cited by Esdaile, without imprint, from an imperfect copy in the Bodleian Library. Caxton's version. The fourteenth of eighteen editions of the fables in English during the period up to 1640. —Arbitrarily dated by being placed here.)

GREENE, ROBERT. Ciceronis amor. W. Stansby for J. Smethwicke. (STC 12229. Seventh edition.)

GREENE, ROBERT. Greenes Never too late. For J. Smethwicke. (Esdaile. Fifth edition.)

TARLTON, RICHARD. Tarltons jests, drawn into three parts. J. H. (Esdaile. First edition.)

CERVANTES SAAVEDRA, MIGUEL DE. The history of the valorous and wittie knight-errant, Don-Quixote of the Mancha. Translated out of the Spanish [by Thomas Shelton]. W. Stansby for E. Blount and W. Barret. (STC 4915. First edition. —Part 1 only; for part 2 see 1620.)

DELONEY, THOMAS. Thomas of Reading. Now the fourth time corrected and enlarged. By T. D. For T. P. (STC 6569. This edition, presumably the fourth, is the earliest known; first edition probably appeared ca.1598.)

JOHNSON, RICHARD. The most famous history of the seven champions of Christendome. T. Snodham. [1612] (STC 14680. Third edition.)

LODGE, THOMAS. Euphues golden legacie. For J. Smethwick. (STC 16670. Eighth edition.)

MANDEVILLE, Sir JOHN. The voyages and travailes of Sir John Mandevile Knight. T. Snodham. (Esdaile; Library of Congress. Seventh edition; earlier editions dated [1496], 1499, [1501?], 1503, 1568, [1583?].)

MERVINE. The most famous and renowned historie, of that woorthie and illustrious knight Mervine. By I. M. Gent. R. Blower and V. Sims. (STC 17844. Probably the second edition; entered SR in 1596. —Translated from the French, possibly by Gervase Markham.)

ROBERTS, HENRY. Haigh for Devonshire. T. Creede. (STC 21081a. Second edition.)

1613

ANTON, ROBERT. Moriomachia. S. Stafford. STC 685)

B., A., *of physicke doctor*. The merie tales of the mad men of Gotham. Cited, without imprint, by Hazlitt. No copy known. Second edition? First edition dates ca.1565. —Ascribed to Andrew Borde.)

HALL, JOSEPH. The discovery of a new world. By an English Mercury. For E. Blount, and W. Barrett. [1613?] (Second edition; cf. the edition of Hall's work made by H. Brown, 1937, pp. xxx-xxxi. —Translated from the Latin by John Healey.)

LYLY, JOHN. Euphues. The anatomy of wit. For W. Leake. (STC 17063. Sixteenth edition.)

LYLY, JOHN. Euphues and his England. For W. Leake. (Huntington Library. Fifteenth edition.)

MARKHAM, GERVASE. The second and last part of the first booke of the English Arcadia. By G. M. N. Okes for T. Saunders. (STC 17352. Part 1 appeared in 1607.)

PETTIE, GEORGE. A petite pallace of Pettie his pleasure. G. Eld. (STC 19823. Seventh edition.)

SCOGGIN, JOHN. Scoggins jestes. R. Blower. (STC 21851. A quite different version appeared in 1626.)

SIDNEY, Sir PHILIP. The Countesse of Pembrokes Arcadia. Now the fourth time published. H. L. for S. Waterson. (STC 2244. Sixth edition. —Another issue of this edition has imprint: H. L. for M. Lownes. [STC 22544a].)

TARLTON, RICHARD. Tarltons jests. Drawne into these three parts.

For J. Budge. (Folger Library. Second edition.)

1614

COBBLER OF CANTERBURY. The merry tales of the cobler of Canterburie. For N. Butter. (Esdaile; Huntington Library. Third edition.)

GREENE, ROBERT. Pandosto, the triumph of time. T. C. for G. Potter, sold J. Tap. (STC 12289. Sixth edition.)

LODGE, THOMAS. Euphues golden legacie. For J. Smethwicke. (STC 16671. Ninth edition.)

1615

FORDE, EMANUEL. Parismus, the renoumed Prince of Bohemia. T. Creede. (STC 11173. Third edition.)

GREENE, ROBERT. Philomela, the Lady Fitzwaters nightingale. G. Purslowe. (STC 12297. Second edition; first edition in 1592.)

JACK OF DOVER. Jacke of Dovers merry tales. Or his quest of inquiry. J. B., sold by R. Higgenbotham. (STC 14292. Third edition.)

PALMERIN D'OLIVA. Palmerin d'Oliva: turned into English by A[nthony] M[unday]. T. Creede. (STC 19159. Third edition; earlier editions in 1588, 1597.)

1616

FAUCONBRIDGE, GEORGE, Lord. The famous history of George Lord Fauconbridge, bastard son to Richard Cordelion. J. B., sold by J. Davies. (STC 10709. First edition.)

11

GAINSFORD, THOMAS. The historie of Trebizond. For T. Downe and E. Dawson. (STC 11521. —Some copies have variant imprint: For T. Downes and E. Dawson.)

GREENE, ROBERT. Ciceronis amor. W. Stansby for J. Smethwicke. (STC 12230. Eighth edition.)

GREENE, ROBERT. Greenes Groatsworth of wit. (Cited by Esdaile, without imprint, from the *Censura Literaria*. Fourth edition.)

GREENE, ROBERT. Greenes Mourning garment. G. Purslowe. (STC 12252. Third edition; earlier editions in 1590, 1597.)

GREENE, ROBERT. Greenes never too late. W. Stansby for J. Smithwicke. (STC 12256. Sixth edition.)

GREENE, ROBERT. Greenes Arcadia, or Menaphon. W. Stansby for J. Smethwicke. (STC 12275. Fifth edition.)

P A L M E R I N D'OLIVA. Palmerin d'Oliva. T. C. and B. A. for R. Higgenbotham. (STC 19159a. Fourth edition.)

PALMERIN OF ENGLAND. The first [-second] part . . . of the famous and fortunate Prince Palmerin of England. Translated out of French, by A[nthony] M[unday]. T. Creede, and B. Alsop. (STC 19163. Third edition.)

1617

AESOP. Esops Eables [sic] translated grammatically [by John Brinsley]. H. L. for T. Man. (Huntington Library. First appearance of this version, intended as a school text; the fifteenth of eighteen editions of the fables in English during the period up to 1640.)

GREENE, ROBERT. Alcida Greenes Metamorphosis. G. Purslowe. (STC 12216. Second edition?; entered SR 1588.)

GREENE, ROBERT. Arbasto, the anatomie of fortune. J. B. for R. Jackson. (STC 12221. Fourth edition; earlier editions in 1584 (2 issues), 1589, 1594.)

GREENE, ROBERT. Greens Farewell to follie. W. White. (STC 12242. Second edition; first edition in 1591.)

GREENE, ROBERT. Greenes Groatsworth of witte. B. Alsop, for H. Bell. STC 12247. Fifth edition.)

LEFEVRE, RAOUL. The ancient historie of the destruction of Troy. The fifth edition. B. Alsop. (STC 15381. Seventh edition.)

LYLY, JOHN. Euphues. [Both parts.] G. Eld, for W. B., sold A. Johnson. (STC 17064. First edition of both parts together.)

ROBERTS, HENRY. The historie of Pheander the mayden knight. The fourth edition. B. Alsop. (STC 21087. Fourth edition; first edition in 1595; nothing is known of any second or third edition.)

S., N. Merry jests, concerning popes, monkes, and friers. Written first in Italian by N. S. and thence translated into French by G. I. and out of French into English, by R[owland] W[illet]. G. Eld. (STC 21510)

1618

AMADIS DE GAULE. Amadis de Gaule. [Books 3 and 4.] Translated into English by A[nthony] M[unday]. N. Okes. (STC 543. First edition of this part. —Books 1 and 2 of this edition appeared in 1619.)

C., W. The first [-second] part of the renowned history of Fragosa King of Aragon. B. A. for G. F. (STC 4319-4320)

FAUST. The historie of the damnable life and deserved death of Dr. John Faustus. E. All-de for E. White. (STC 10713. Third edition.)

MANDEVILLE, Sir JOHN. The voyages and travailes of Sir John Mandevile knight. T. S. (STC 17252. Eighth edition.)

1619

AMADIS DE GAULE. The ancient, famous and honourable history of Amadis de Gaule. [Books 1 and 2.] [Translated by Anthony Munday.] N. Okes. (STC 544. Second edition of these books; first editions in [1590?] and 1595 respectively. —Books 3 and 4 of this edition appeared in 1618.)

CERVANTES SAAVEDRA, MIGUEL DE. The travels of Persiles and Sigismunda. H. L. for M. L. (STC 4918)

DELONEY, THOMAS. The pleasant history of John Winchcomb, in his younger yeares called Jack of Newberie. Now the eight time imprinted. H. Lownes. (STC 6559. Presumably the eighth edition; none earlier known; entered SR 1597.)

FORDE, EMANUEL. The most pleasant historie of Ornatus and Artesia. B. Alsop. (STC 11169a. Third edition.)

GREENE, ROBERT. Pandosto, the triumph of time. E. Allde. (Esdaile; Huntington Library. Seventh edition.)

GRISELDA. The antient true, and admirable history of Patient Grisel. Now translated into English [from French].

H. L. for W. Lugger. (STC 12383. Second edition.)

PRIMALEON OF GREECE. The famous and renowned historie of Primaleon of Greece. Translated out of French and Italian, into English, by A[nthony] M[unday]. T. Snodham. STC 20367. Second edition of parts 1 and 2; first editions in 1595, 1596 respectively. First appearance of part 3.)

1620

BOCCACCIO, GIOVANNI. The Decameron containing an hundred pleasant novels. I. Jaggard. 2v. (STC 3172. First edition.)

CERVANTES SAAVEDRA, MIGUEL DE. The history of Don-Quichote. The first [-second] parte. For E. Blounte. (STC 4916-4917. Second edition of part 1; first edition of part 2. Part 1 is undated. —Translated by Thomas Shelton.)

GESTA ROMANORUM. A record of ancient histories, entituled in Latine: Gesta Romanorum. W. Stansby. [1620?] (STC 21290. Tenth edition.)

GREENE, ROBERT. Greenes Never too late. For J. Smethwicke. [1620?] (STC 12256a. Seventh edition.)

MAINWARINGE, M. Vienna: no art can cure this hart. N. Okes for J. Pyper. (Hazlitt, H. 438. First edition. —A re-working of the old romance of *Paris and Vienne*.)

MEG OF WESTMINSTER. The life of Long Meg of Westminster. E. All-de for E. White. (Esdaile. First known edition; the supposed 1582 edition is spurious.)

PEELE, GEORGE. Merrie conceited jests, of George Peele Gentleman. For

H. Bell. [1620?]   (STC 19542. Second edition.)

REYNARD THE FOX.   The most delectable history of Reynard the Fox. E. Allde.   (STC 20923. Eighth edition; earlier editions in [1481], [1489], [1494], [1515?], 1550, 1560, 1586.

RUSH, FRIAR.   The historie of Frier Rush. E. All-de.   (STC 21451. First edition known; entered SR 1569.)

URFE, HONORE D'.   The history of Astrea. The first part. Newly translated out of French. N. Okes for J. Pyper.   (STC 24525)

WESTWARD FOR SMELTS.   Westward for smelts. Or, The water-mans fare of mad-merry western wenches. Written by Kinde Kit of Kingstone. For J. Trundle.   (STC 25292)

1621

AUDIGUIER, VITAL D'.   Lisander and Calista, a tragi-comical history. (Cited by Esdaile, without imprint, from Hazlitt. First edition.)

GREENE, ROBERT.   Greenes Groatsworth of witte. N. O. for H. Bell. STC 12248. Sixth edition.)

I., R.   The history of Tom Thumbe. For T. Langley.   (STC 14056. Ascribed to Richard Johnson.)

MAINWARINGE, M.   The honour of true love and knighthood, wherein are storied the noble atchievements of Sir Paris of Vienna and the faire Princesse Vienna. B. Alsop.   (Esdaile. Second edition of this version; no copy known.)

REYNOLDS, JOHN.   The triumphs of Gods revenege [sic]. F. Kyngston, for W. Lee.   (STC 20942. First edition. — Part 1 only; for parts 2 and 3 of this edition, see 1622 and 1624.)

SIDNEY, Sir PHILIP.   The Countesse of Pembrokes Arcadia. Now the fift time published. Also a supplement of a defect in the third part of this history. By Sir W. Alexander. Dublin: Society of Stationers.   (STC 22545. Seventh edition.)

SIDNEY, Sir PHILIP.   The Countesse of Pembrokes Arcadia. H. L. for S. Waterson.   (University of Illinois Library. Eighth edition.)

VEGA CARPIO, LOPE DE.   The pilgrim of Casteele. J. Norton.   (STC 25629. First edition.)

WROTH, Lady MARY.   The Countesse of Mountgomeries Urania. For J. Marriott and J. Grismand.   (STC 26051)

1622

ALEMAN, MATEO.   The rogue: or The life of Guzman de Alfarache. Written in Spanish. For E. Blount. STC 288. First edition.)

CESPEDES Y MENESES, GONZALO. Gerardo the unfortunate Spaniard. Originally in Spanish, and made English by L[eonard] D[igges]. For E. Blount.   (STC 4919. First edition.)

FAUST.   The historie of the damnable life and deserved death of Dr. John Faustus.   (Cited by Esdaile, without imprint, from the Harleian catalogue. Fourth edition.)

HELIODORUS.   Heliodorus his Aethiopian history: done out of Greeke. F. Kyngston, for W. Barret.   (STC 13046. Sixth edition. —Translated by Thomas Underdowne, revised by Barret.)

LUNA, JUAN DE.   The pursuit of the Historie of Lazarillo de Tormez. And now done into English. B. Alsop for

14

T. Walkley. (STC 16927. First edition.)

REYNOLDS, JOHN. The triumphs of Gods revenge. Booke II. F. Kyngston, for W. Lee. (STC 20942. Part 2 only: for parts 1 and 3 of this edition see 1621 and 1624.)

REYNOLDS, JOHN. The triumphs of Gods revenge. Booke II. A. Mathewes for W. Lee. (STC 20943. Part 2 only; for parts 1 and 3 of this (2d) edition see 1629 and 1623.)

SIDNEY, Sir PHILIP. The Countesse of Pembrokes Arcadia. Now the sixt time published. H. L. for Mathew Lownes. (STC 22546. Ninth edition; some copies have date 1623 in imprint.)

1623

ALEMAN, MATEO. The rogue: or The life of Guzman de Alfarache. For E. Blount. (STC 289. Second issue of the first (1622) edition.)

DELONEY, THOMAS. Thomas of Reading. Now the fift time corrected and enlarged. W. J. for T. P. (STC 6570. Fifth edition.)

JOHNSON, RICHARD. The most famous history of the seven champions of Christendome. Sold by R. Dainell. (STC 14681. Fourth edition.)

LODGE, THOMAS. Euphues golden legacie. For J. Smethwicke. (STC 16672. Tenth edition.)

LYLY, JOHN. Euphues. [Both parts.] J. Beale, for J. Parker. (STC 17065. Second edition of both parts together.)

REYNOLDS, JOHN. The triumphs of Gods revenge. Booke. III. A. Mathewes, for W. Lee. (STC 20943. Part

3 only; for parts 1 and 2 of this (2d) edition see 1629 and 1622.)

SIDNEY, Sir PHILIP. The Countesse of Pembrokes Arcadia. Now the sixt time published. H. L. for M. Lownes. (STC 22546a. Second issue of the ninth (1622) edition.)

VEGA CARPIO, LOPE DE. The pilgrim of Casteele. Written in Spanish. E. All-de for J. N., sold by T. Dewe. (STC 24630. Second edition. —Some copies have imprint: London, Printed. Anno Dom. 1623.)

1624

AESOP. Esops Fables translated both grammatically, and also in propriety of our English phrase [by John Brinsley]. J. D. for T. Man. (STC 188. Second edition of Brinsley's version; the sixteenth of eighteen editions of the fables in English during the period up to 1640.)

BELING, RICHARD. A sixth booke to the Countesse of Pembrokes Arcadia. Written by R. B. Esq. Dublin: Societie of Stationers. (STC 1805. Forms part of the text in all editions of the *Arcadia* beginning with that of 1627.)

LAZARILLO DE TORMES. The pleasant history of Lazarillo de Tormes. Drawn out of Spanish, by David Rowland. J. H. (STC 15338. Fourth edition; earlier editions in 1576, 1586, 1596.)

MORE, Sir THOMAS. Sir Thomas Moore's Utopia. Translated into English by R. Robinson. B. Alsop. (STC 18097. Fifth edition.)

REYNOLDS, JOHN. The triumphs of Gods revenge. Booke III. F. Kyngston for W. Lee. (STC 20942. Part 3

only; for pts. 1 and 2 of this (1st)
edition see 1621 and 1622.)

1625

BARCLAY, JOHN. Barclay his Argenis. Translated out of Latine into English, by Kingesmill Long, Gent. G. P. for H. Seile. (STC 1392. First edition.)

BOCCACCIO, G I O V A N N I. The modell of wit, mirth, eloquence, and conversation. Framed in ten dayes . . . And now translated into English. I. Jaggard, for M. Lownes. 2v. (STC 3173. Second edition; the second volume is the same as that issued with the 1620 edition, and hence has title beginning: *The Decameron*, and imprint date of 1620.)

MANDEVILLE, Sir JOHN. The voyages and travailes of Sir John Mandevile knight. T. Snodham. (STC 17253. Ninth edition.)

1626

BACON, Sir FRANCIS. New Atlantis. In: Sylva sylvarum. J. H. for W. Lee. STC 1168. First edition.)

BERNARD, RICHARD. The isle of man. For E. Blackmore. (STC 1946. First edition.)

CARTIGNY, JEAN DE. The voyage of the wandring knight. Translated out of French into English, by W[illiam] G[oodyear]. W. Stansby. [1626?] (STC 4703. Fourth edition.)

DELONEY, THOMAS. The pleasant historie of John Winchcomb, in his yonguer yeares called Jack of Newbery. Now the tenth time imprinted. H. Lownes, sold by C. Wright. (STC 6560. Ninth edition.)

GREENE, R O B E R T. Arbasto, the anatomy of fortune. Whereunto is

added a lovely poem of Pyramus and Thisbe. For F. Williams. (STC 12222. Fifth edition.)

JOHNSON, RICHARD. The famous historie of the seaven champions of Christendome. W. Stansby. 2 pts. (STC 14682. Fifth edition; pt.2 has separate title-page, with imprint: R. Bishop.)

RUSH, FRIAR. The historie of Friar Rush. E. All-de, sold by F. Grove. (STC 21452. Second edition.)

SCOGGIN, JOHN. The first and best part of Scoggins jests. Gathered by Andrew Boord. For F. Williams. (STC 21852. Second edition?; entered SR 1565/6. —Another version appeared in 1613.)

1627

AUDIGUIER, VITAL D'. A tragicomicall history of our times, under the borrowed names of Lisander, and Calista. H. L. for G. Lathum. (STC 906. Second edition.)

BACON, Sir FRANCIS. New Atlantis. (In: Sylva sylvarum. J. H. for W. Lee. STC 1169. Reissue of first edition.)

BACON, ROGER. The famous historie of Fryer Bacon. G. P. for F. Grove. (STC 1183. First edition.)

BERNARD, RICHARD. The isle of man. G. M. for E. Blackemoore. (Folger Library. Probably second or third edition.)

BERNARD, RICHARD. The isle of man. The fourth edition much enlarged. E. Blackmore. (STC 1947. Fourth edition.)

DELONEY, THOMAS. A discourse containing many matters of delight . . . called The gentle craft. For E.

Brewster. (Esdaile. Second edition of part 1; first edition in 1598.)

HELIODORUS. Heliodorus his Aethiopian history. F. Kyngston for W. Barret. (Esdaile. Seventh edition. —Translated by Thomas Underdowne, and revised by Barret.)

PEELE, GEORGE. Merrie conceited jests: of George Peele gentleman. G. P. for F. Faulkner. (STC 19543. Third edition.)

PEELE, GEORGE. Merrie conceited jests: of George Peele gentleman. For H. Bell. (STC 19544. Fourth edition.)

SIDNEY, Sir PHILIP. The Countesse of Pembrokes Arcadia. Now the sixt time published. W. S. for S. Waterson. (STC 22547. Tenth edition. —With this is incorporated Beling's *Sixth Booke*, which has separate title-page dated 1628.)

1628

AESOP. The Fables of Esop, in English. Whereunto is added the Fables of Avian: and also the Fables of Alphonce, with the Fables of Poge. For A. Heb. (STC 183. Caxton's version; the seventeenth of eighteen editions of the fables in English published during the period up to 1640.)

BACON, Sir FRANCIS. New Atlantis. (In: Sylva sylvarum. J. H. for W. Lee. STC 1170. Second edition.)

BARCLAY, JOHN. John Barclay his Argenis, translated out of Latine into English: the prose by Sir Robert Le Grys, and the verses by Thomas May. F. Kyngston for R. Meighen and H. Seile. (STC 1393. First edition of this translation; Long's translation appeared in 1625.)

BERNARD, RICHARD. The isle of man. The fifth edition. For E. Blackmore. (STC 1948. Fifth edition.)

GOODFELLOW, ROBIN. Robin Good-fellow, his mad prankes. For F. Grove. (STC 12016. First edition.)

GREENE, ROBERT. Ciceronis amor. W. Stansby for J. Smethwicke. (STC 12231. Ninth edition.)

HIPOLITO. The true history of the tragicke loves of Hipolito and Isabella Neapolitans. Englished. T. Harper, and N. Field. (STC 13516. First edition. —A translation from the French of one Meslier (first name apparently unknown), possibly by Alexander Hart.)

MAINWARINGE, M. Vienna noe art can cure this hart. For G. Percivall. (STC 17201. Undated; third (?) edition of this reworking of the old romance of *Paris and Vienne*.)

1629

BACON, ROGER. The famous historie of Fryer Bacon. E. A. for F. Grove. (STC 1184. Second edition.)

BACON, ROGER. The famous historie of Fryer Bacon. E. A. for F. Grove. (Esdaile. Imprint same as in preceding entry but lacks date; arbitrarily dated by being placed here. Third edition.)

BARCLAY, JOHN. John Barclay his Argenis, translated out of Latine into English: the prose by Sir Robert Le Grys, and the verses by Thomas May. F. Kyngston for R. Meighen and H. Seile. (STC 1394. Second edition of this translation.)

GREENE, ROBERT. Greenes Groatsworth of wit. J. Haviland for H. Bell. (STC 12249. Seventh edition.)

17

GREENE, ROBERT. Pandosto, the triumph of time. T. P. for F. Faulkner. (STC 12290. Eighth edition.)

PASQUIL. Pasquils jests, mixed with Mother Bunches merriments. M. F., sold by F. Grove. (STC 19452. Third edition.)

REYNARD THE FOX. The most delectable history of Reynard the Fox. E. All-de. (STC 20924. Ninth edition.)

REYNOLDS, JOHN. The triumphes of Gods revenge. The first booke. A. Mathewes for W. Lee. (STC 20943. Second edition, part 1 only; for parts 2 and 3 of this edition see 1622 and 1623.)

RUSH, FRIAR. The history of Frier Rush. E. All-de. (Folger Library title-page only). Third edition.)

SIDNEY, Sir PHILIP. The Countesse of Pembrokes Arcadia. Now the seventh time published. H. L. and R. Y., sold by S. Waterson. (STC 22548. Eleventh edition. —Beling's *Sixth booke* has separate title-page dated 1628.)

1630

ALEMAN, MATEO. The rogue: or, The life of Guzman de Alfarache. Oxford: W. Turner, for R. Allot. (STC 290. Second edition.)

B., A. The merry tales of the mad men of Gotham. B. A. and T. F. for M. Sparke. (STC 1021. Fourth edition? (there is record of a fine collected in 1619 for a pirated edition). —Ascribed to Andrew Borde.)

BERNARD, RICHARD. The isle of man. The seventh edition. For E. Blackmore. (STC 1949. Seventh edition.)

C., S. The famous and delectable history of Cleocreton & Cloryana. J. B. for C. Tyus. (STC 4302. Undated; although the STC places this work in this year, it is likely that a date of ca. 1660 is more nearly correct.)

COBBLER OF CANTERBURY. The tincker of Turvey. For N. Butter. (STC 4581. Fourth edition; earlier editions appeared under title: *The Cobler of Caunterburie.*)

DELONEY, THOMAS. The pleasant history of John Winchcomb, in his younger yeares called Jack of Newberie. The eleventh edition. H. L. and R. Y., sold by J. Harrigat. (STC 6561. The tenth edition.)

FORDE, EMANUEL. The most famous, delectable, and pleasant historie of Parismus. B. Alsop and T. Fawcet, sold by T. Alchorn. 2v. (STC 11174. Fourth edition.)

GREENE, ROBERT. Greenes Never too late. For J. Smethwicke. [1630?] (STC 12257a. Eighth edition?; probably same as STC 12256a, [1620?]. —STC 12257 is a ghost entry.)

LYLY, JOHN. Euphues. [Both parts.] J. H., sold by J. Boler. (Esdaile. Third edition of both parts. —Some copies are dated 1631 [STC 17066].)

TARLTON, RICHARD. Tarltons newes out of Purgatory. G. Purslowe, sold by F. Grove. (STC 23686. Second edition; first edition in 1590.)

1631

BACON, Sir FRANCIS. New Atlantis. (In: Sylva sylvarum. J. H. for W. Lee. STC 1171. Third edition.)

BREWER, THOMAS. The life and death of the merry devill of Edmonton. T. P. for F. Faulkner. (STC 3719)

GREENE, ROBERT. Greenes Never too late. W. Stansby for J. Smithwicke. (STC 12258. Ninth edition.)

GREENE, ROBERT. Philomela, the Lady Fitz-Waters nightingale. G. Purslowe. (STC 12298. Third edition.)

JOHNSON, RICHARD. The most pleasant history of Tom a Lincolne. The sixth impression. A. Mathewes, sold by R. Byrde, and F. Coules. (STC 14684. Sixth edition (earliest extant); entered SR 1599.)

LUNA, JUAN DE. The pursuit of the Historie of Lazarillo de Tormez. G. P. for R. Hawkins. (STC 16928. Second edition.)

LYLY, JOHN. Euphues. [Both parts.] J. H., sold by J. Boler. (STC 17066. Fourth edition of both parts; some copies are dated 1630.)

1632

BERNARD, RICHARD. The isle of Man. The eight edition. G. M. for E. Blackmore. (STC 1950. Eighth edition.)

BIONDI, GIOVANNI FRANCESCO. Eromena, or, Love and revenge. Written originally in the Thoscan tongue and new faithfully Englished, by Ja. Hayward. R. Badger, for R. Allot. (STC 3075)

DELONEY, THOMAS. Thomas of Reading. Now the sixth time corrected and enlarged. E. Allde for R. Bird. (STC 6571. Sixth edition.)

FORTUNATE LOVERS. The fortunate, the deceived, and the unfortunate lovers. (Cited by Esdaile, without imprint, from Scott.)

GOODMAN, NICHOLAS. Hollands Leaguer. A. M. for R. Barnes. (STC 12027)

GREEN, GEORGE A. The pinder of Wakefield: being the merry history of George a Greene. G. P. for E. Blackamoore. (STC 12213. Only edition; the 1633 edition in Esdaile is in error.)

GREENE, ROBERT. Pandosto, the triumph of time. For F. Faulkner. (STC 12291. Ninth edition.)

MAINWARINGE, M. Vienna. Noe art can cure this hart. For R. Hawkins. (STC 17202. Undated; fourth (?) edition of this re-working of the old romance of *Paris and Vienne*.)

MANDEVILLE, Sir JOHN. The voyages and travailes of Sir John Mandevile knight. W. Stansby. (Yale University Library. Tenth edition.)

PASQUIL. Pasquils jests: with the merriments of Mother Bunch. M. F. sold F. Coles. (STC 19453. Fourth edition.)

1633

DELONEY, THOMAS. The pleasant history of John Winchcomb, in his younger yeares called Jack of Newberie. Now the ninth time imprinted. R. Young, sold by C. Wright. (STC 6562. Eleventh edition.)

FORDE, EMANUEL. The famous historie of Montelyon, Knight of the Oracle. B. Alsop and T. Fawcet. (STC 11167. First edition known.)

HIPOLITO. The true history of the tragicke loves of Hipolito and Isabella Neapolitans. The second edition. T. Harper, sold R. Meighen. (STC 13517. Second edition.)

SEVEN SAGES. The hystorie of the seaven wise maisters of Rome. T. Purfoote. (STC 21300. Fifth edition.)

SIDNEY, Sir PHILIP. The Countesse of Pembrokes Arcadia. Now the eighth time published. For S. Waterson and R. Young. (STC 22549. Twelfth edition.)

1634

AESOP. The Fables of Esop, in English. J. H. for A. Hebb. (STC 184. Caxton's version; the last of eighteen editions of the fables in English during the period up to 1640.)

ALEMAN, MATEO. The rogue: or, The life of Guzman de Alfarache. The third edition. R. B. for R. Allot. (STC 291. Third edition. —Title-page to part 2 is dated 1633.)

BERNARD, RICHARD. The isle of man. The ninth edition. G. M. for E. Blackmore. (Folger Library. Ninth edition.)

BOCCACCIO, GIOVANNI. The modell of wit, mirth, eloquence, and conversation. Framed in ten dayes. The third edition. T. Cotes, sold by B. Allen, and W. Hope. (STC 3174. Third edition.)

C., N. A Saxon historie, of the admirable adventures of Clodoaldus and his three children. Translated out of French, by Sr. T. H[awkins]. E. P. for H. Seile. (STC 4294)

CACOETHES. Cacoethes leaden legacie: or His schoole of ill manners. For T. Lambert. [1634] (STC 4326)

FORDE, EMANUEL. The most pleasant history of Ornatus and Artesia. B. Alsop and T. Fawcet. (STC 11170. Fourth edition.)

GREENE, ROBERT. Euphues his censure to Philautus. E. All-de. (STC 12240. Second edition; first edition in 1587.)

GREENE, ROBERT. Greenes Arcadia, or Menaphon. (Cited by Esdaile, without imprint, from the *Censura Literaria*. Sixth edition.)

JOHNSON, RICHARD. The pleasant conceites of Old Hobson, the merry Londoner. For J. Wright. (Esdaile. Third edition.)

LODGE, THOMAS. Euphues golden legacie. For J. Smethwicke. (STC 16673. Eleventh edition. —Pforzheimer copy has variant imprint: For F. Smethwicke.)

LUCIAN. Certaine select dialogues of Lucian: together with his True historie, translated by Mr Francis Hickes. Oxford: W. Turner. (STC 16893)

MALORY, Sir THOMAS. The most ancient and famous history of the renowned Prince Arthur King of Britaine. W. Stansby, for J. Bloome. (STC 806. Seventh edition of Malory's work; earlier editions in 1485, 1498, 1529, [1557], [1585?], with a sixth undated.)

1635

AUDIGUIER, VITAL D'. A tragicomicall history of our times, under the borrowed names of Lisander and Calista. R. Y. for G. Latham. (STC 907. Third edition.)

BACON, Sir FRANCIS. New Atlantis. (In: Sylva sylvarum. J. Haviland for W. Lee, sold by J. Williams. STC 1172. Fourth edition.)

BERNARD, RICHARD. The isle of man. The tenth edition. J. H. for E. Blackmore. (STC 1951. Tenth edition.)

BIONDI, GIOVANNI FRANCESCO. Donzella desterrada, or The banish'd virgin. Written originally in Italian, and Englished by J[ames] H[ayward]. T. Cotes, for H. Mosley. (STC 3074)

DELONEY, THOMAS. A discourse containing many matters of delight. The gentle craft. (Cited by Esdaile, without imprint, from the Harleian catalogue. Third edition.)

FAUCONBRIDGE, GEORGE, Lord. The famous history of George Lord Fauconbridge bastard son of Richard Cordelion. J. B., sold J. Wright jr. (STC 10710. Second edition.)

JOHNSON, RICHARD. The most pleasant history of Tom a Lincolne. The seventh impression. A. M., sold by F. Faulkner, and F. Coules. (STC 14685. Seventh edition.)

MEG OF WESTMINSTER. The life of Long Meg of Westminster. For R. Bird. (STC 17783. Second edition.)

PASQUIL. Pasquils jests, mixed with Mother Bunches merriments. M. Flesher, sold by A. Kembe. (Capell Collection. Fifth edition.)

REYNOLDS, JOHN. The triumphs of Gods revenge. For W. Lee. (STC 20944. First appearance of parts 4-6; third edition of parts 1-3.)

SILESIO, MARIANO, pseud. The Arcadian princesse; or, The triumph of justice. Faithfully rendred to the originall Italian copy, by Ri. Brathwait Esq. T. Harper for R. Bostocke. (STC 22553. Probably written by Brathwait.)

1636

BARCLAY, JOHN. Barclay his Argenis. Faithfully translated out of Latin into English. By Kingsmill Long. The second edition. For H. Seile. (STC 1395. Second edition of this translation.)

BETTIE, W. The historie of Titana, and Theseus. For R. Bird. (STC 1981. Second edition.)

DELONEY, THOMAS. Thomas of Reading. For R. Bird. (STC 6572. Seventh edition.)

DESMARETS DE ST. SORLIN, JEAN. Ariana. Translated out of the French. J. Haviland, for T. Walkley. (STC 6779. First edition.)

FAUST. The historie of the damnable life, and deserved death of Doctor John Faustus. Translated into English by P. R. Gent. For J. Wright. (STC 10714. Fifth edition.)

FORDE, EMANUEL. The most famous, delectable, and pleasant historie of Parismus. B. Alsop and T. Fawcet. 2v. (STC 11175. Fifth edition.)

GREENE, ROBERT. The pleasant historie of Dorastus and Fawnia. For F. Faulkner. (STC 12292. Tenth edition; earlier editions appeared under title: *Pandosto.*)

LEFEVRE, RAOUL. The anient historie of the destruction of Troy. The sixth edition. B. Alsop and T. Fawcet. STC 15382. Eighth edition.)

LYLY, JOHN. Euphues. [Both parts.] J. Haviland. (STC 17067. Fifth edition of both parts.)

MEG OF WESTMINSTER. The life of Long Meg of Westminster. For R. Bird. (Esdaile. Third edition.)

1637

DELONEY, THOMAS. The gentle craft. For R. Bird. (STC 6555. Fourth edition.)

DELONEY, THOMAS. The pleasant history of John Winchcomb, in his younger yeares called Jack of Newberie. Now the tenth time imprinted. R. Young, sold by C. Wright. (STC 6563. Twelfth edition.)

GREENE, ROBERT. Greene's Groastworth of wit. For H. and M. Bell. (STC 12250. Eighth edition.)

PALMERIN D'OLIVA. Palermin d'Oliva. The first [-second] part. Turned into English by A[nthony] M[unday]. B. Alsop and T. Fawcet. STC 19160. Fifth edition.)

SUMMERS, WILL. A pleasant history of the life and death of Will Summers. J. Okes, sold by F. Grove and T. Lambart. (Folger Library. First edition.)

VALENTINE AND ORSON. Valentine and Orson. The two sonnes of the Emperour of Greece. T. Purfoot. (STC 24573. Fourth edition. —An abridgement.)

HISTOIRE. Histoire des larrons, or The history of theeves. Written in French, and translated by Paul Godwin. J. Raworth, sold by T. Slater. (STC 13523. —French original attributed to François de Calvi.)

SIDNEY, Sir PHILIP. The Countesse of Pembrokes Arcadia. Now the ninth time published, with a twofold supplement of a defect in the third book: the one by Sr W. A[lexander], the other by Mr Ja. Johnstoun. For J. Waterson and R. Young. (STC 22550. Thirteenth edition.)

STUKELEY. The famous history of Stout Stukley. R. J. for F. Grove. (Esdaile. —Entered SR 11 May 1638.)

TARLTON, RICHARD. Tarltons jests. Drawne into these three parts. J. H. for A. Crook. (STC 23684. Third edition.)

1638

ACHILLES TATIUS. The loves of Clitophon and Leucippe. Now Englished [by Anthony Hodges.] Oxford: W. Turner for J. Allam. (STC 91. First edition of this translation; earlier translation by W. Burton, 1597.)

AUDIGUIER, VITAL D'. Love and valour: celebrated in the person of the author, by the name of Adraste. Translated out of the French by W. B[arwick]. T. Harper, for T. Slater. (STC 905)

GARCIA, CARLOS. The sonne of the rogue, or The politick theefe. Now Englished by W[illiam] M[elvin]. J. D., sold by B. Langford. (STC 11550. —Some copies have imprint: . . . sold by G. Hutton.)

GODWIN, FRANCIS. The man in the moone. J. Norton, for J. Kirton and T. Warren. (STC 11943)

1639

APULEIUS. The xi. bookes of the Golden Asse. Translated out of Latine into English, by William Adlington. T. Harper, for T. Alchorn. (STC 721. Fifth edition; earlier editions in 1566, 1571, 1582, 1596.)

BACON, Sir FRANCIS. New Atlantis. (In: Sylva sylvarum. J. H. for W. Lee. STC 1173. Fifth edition.)

BOISROBERT, FRANCOIS LE METEL DE. [The history of Annaxander and Orazia. An Indian story. Translated out of French into English by William Duncombe.] (Esdaile. —Licensed to S. Waterson in 1639; no copy known.)

CAMUS, JEAN PIERRE. Admirable events: selected out of foure bookes, written in French by John Peter Camus. Together with Morall relations, written by the same author. And translated into English by S. Du Verger. T. Harper for W. Brooks. (STC 4549. —Part 2 translated by Thomas Brugis. —Another issue, same year: T. Harper, for A. Roper. [STC 4550].)

DELONEY, THOMAS. The gentle craft. The second part. E. Purslow. STC 6556).

GESTA ROMANORUM. A record of ancient histories entituled in Latine: Gesta Romanorum. R. Bishop. [1639] (STC 21290a. Eleventh edition.)

GOMBAULD, JEAN O G I E R DE. Endimion. Now elegantly interpreted, by Richard Hurst Gentleman. J. Okes. for S. Browne. (STC 11991)

GOODFELLOW, R O B I N. Robin Good-Fellow, his mad prankes and merry jests. T. Cotes, sold by F .Grove. (STC 12107. Second edition.)

GREENE, ROBERT. Ciceronis amor. R. Young for J. Smethwicke. (STC 12232. Tenth edition.)

JOHNSON, RICHARD. The famous history of the seven champions of Christendome. R. Bishop. [1639?] (STC 14683. Sixth edition.)

LAZARILLO DE T O R M E S. The pleasant history of Lazarillo de Tormes. Drawne out of Spanish by David Rowland. The third edition. E. G. for W. Leake. 2 pts. (STC 15339. Fifth edition of part 1; the second part is Luna's *Pursuit,* third edition.)

MORE, Sir THOMAS. The commonwealth of Utopia. B. Alsop & T. Fawcet, sold by W. Sheares. (STC 18098. Sixth edition of Robinson's translation.)

PALMERIN OF E N G L A N D. The first [-second] part of the history of the famous and fortunate Prince Palmerin of England. Translated out of French by A[nthony] M[unday]. B. Alsop and T. Fawcet. (STC 19164. Fourth edition.)

PIUS II. The historie of Eurialus and Lucretia. Written in Latine by Eneas Sylvius; and translated into English by Charles Allen, Gent. T. Cotes, for W. Cooke. (STC 19973. First appearance of this translation.)

REYNOLDS, JOHN. The triumphs of Gods revenge. E. Griffin for W. Lee. (STC 20945. Fourth edition.)

RIVERS, GEORGE. The heroinae: or The lives of Arria, Paulina, Lucrecia, Dido, Theutilla, Cypriana, Aretaphila. R. Bishop, for J. Colby. (STC 21063)

S., J. Clidamas, or The Sicilian tale. T. Payne, sold by J. Cowper. (STC 21501. —Esdaile cites, without imprint, another 1639 edition.)

1640

BACON, ROGER. The famous history of Fryer Bacon. T. C. (Esdaile; Folger Library. Fourth edition.)

BARCLAY, JOHN. An epitome of the history of faire Argenis and Polyarchus, extracted out of the Latin, and put in French. And translated out of the French into English by a yong gentlewoman [i.e. Judith Man]. E. G. for H. Seile. (STC 1396)

BERNARD, RICHARD. The isle of man. The eleventh edition. G. M. for E. Blackmore. (STC 1952. Eleventh edition.)

BRATHWAIT, RICHARD. Ar't asleepe husband? A boulster lecture. By Philogenes Panedonius [pseud.] R. Bishop, for R. B. or his assignes. (STC 3555. —Some copies have imprint: R. Bishop for R. Best.)

BRATHWAIT, RICHARD. The two Lancashire lovers: or The excellent history of Philocles and Doriclea. By Musaeus Palatinus [pseud.] E. Griffin for R. B. or his assignes. (STC 3590. —Another issue, with new title-page and imprint: E. Griffin for R. Best. [STC 3590a].)

CAWWOOD. The pleasant history of Cawwood the rooke. T. C. for F. Grove. (STC 4889. First edition.)

CERVANTES SAAVEDRA, MIGUEL DE. Exemplarie novells; in sixe books. Turned into English by Don Diego Puede-Ser [i.e. James Mabbe]. J. Dawson, for R. M., sold by L. Blaicklocke. (STC 4914)

DELONEY, THOMAS. The gentle craft. For R. Bird. (British Museum. Fifth edition.)

FORDE, EMANUEL. The famous historie of Montelyon, Knight of the Oracle. B. Alsop, and T. Fawcet. (Folger Library. Second known edition.)

GRACIAN DANTISCO, LUCAS. Galateo espagnol, or, The Spanish gallant. Done into English by W[illiam] S[tyle] of the Inner Temple Esquire. E. G. for William Lee. (Contains: "The tale of the great Soldan, and of the loves of the beautiful Axa and the Prince of Naples." pp. 127-152; sig. G10r -H11v.)

GRISELDA. The pleasant and sweet history of patient Grissell. Translated out of Italian. E. P. for J. Wright. (STC 12386. Mixed prose and verse. STC dates the pamphlet [1630?] but from what remains of imprint (largely cut away) 1640 seems the likelier date. For prose version see 1607, 1619.)

HART, ALEXANDER. The tragicomicall history of Alexto and Angelica. B. A. and T. F. for N. Vavasour. (STC 12885)

HOWELL, JAMES. Dendrologia. Dodona's grove, or, The vocall forrest. T. B. for H. Mosley. (STC 13872)

JOHNSON, RICHARD. The pleasant conceites of Old Hobson, the merry Londoner. W. Gilbertson. (Esdaile. Fourth edition.)

MANDEVILLE, Sir JOHN. The voyages and travailes of Sir John Mandevile knight. R. Bishop. [1640?] (STC 17254. Eleventh edition.)

QUEVEDO Y VILLEGAS, FRANCISCO DE. Visions, or, Hels kingdome, and the worlds follies and abuses, strangely displaied by R[ichard] C[roshaw]. E. G. for S. Burton. (STC 20561)

REYNARD THE FOX. The most delectable history of Reynard the Fox. R. Oulton, for J. Wright the younger. (STC 20925. Tenth edition. —Another issue, same year, with imprint: For J. Salter. [STC 20925a].)

REYNOLDS, JOHN. The triumphs of Gods revenge. E. Griffin for W. Lee. (STC 20946. Fifth edition.)

SAULNIER, GILBERT, sieur du VERDIER. The love and armes of the Greeke Princes. Or, The romant of romants. Translated for the Right Honourable, Philip, Earle of Pembroke and Montgomery. T. Harper, for T. Walkley. (STC 21775)

1641

BRATHWAIT, RICHARD. The penitent pilgrim. J. Dawson, sold by J. Williams. (Wing B4275)

24

CAMUS, JEAN PIERRE. Diotrephe. Or, an historie of Valentines. T. Harper. (Wing C412. —Translated by S. Du Verger.)

DESMARETS DE ST. SORLIN, JEAN. Ariana. The second edition. J. Dawson for T. Walkley. (Wing D1194. Second edition.)

JOHNSON, JOHN. The academy of love. For H. Blunden. (Wing J782)

MARIANUS. Marianus, or, Loves heroick champion. B. Aslop and T. Fawcet, sold by J. Becket. (Wing M600)

QUEVEDO Y VILLEGAS, FRANCISCO DE. Hell reformed or a Glasse for favorits. E. Griffin for S. Burton. (Wing Q189. —Translated by Edward Messervy.)

1642

LODGE, THOMAS. Euphues golden legacie. For F. Smethwicke. (Wing L2810. Twelfth edition.)

1643

1644

HOWELL, JAMES. Dendrologia. Dodona's grove, or The vocall forrest. The second edition. [Oxford: H. Hall] (Wing H3059. Second edition.)

1645

CERIZIERS, RENE DE. Innocency acknowledg'd in the life and death of St. Genovefa Countesse Palatin of Trevers. Translated by J[ohn] T[ansborough]. At Garnt: J. van der Kerchoue. (Wing C1678)

HOWELL, JAMES. Dendrologia. Dodona's grove, or The vocall forrest. The third edition. Cambridge: R. D. for H. Moseley. (Wing H3060. Third edition.)

1646

AESOP. Aesop's Fables. I. L. for A. Hebb. (Wing A686. Peacham's version, of which this is the first appearance; the nineteenth of twenty-four editions of the fables in English during the period up to 1660.)

C., W. The first [-second] part of the renowned history of Fragosa King of Aragon. B. Alsop. (Wing C152. Second edition.)

1647

AESOP. The fables of Esop. F. B. for A. Hebb. (Wing A687. Caxton's version; the twentieth of twenty-four editions of the fables in English during the period up to 1660.)

BARON, ROBERT. Erotopaigeion. Or the Cyprian academy. W. W., sold by J. Hardesty, T. Huntington, and T. Jackson. (Wing B889. Re-issued the following year.)

GOMBERVILLE, MARIN LE ROY, sieur de. The history of Polexander. Done into English by William Browne, Gent. T. Harper for T. Walkley. (Wing G1025. First edition.)

MACHIAVELLI, NICCOLO. The divell a married man, or, The divell hath met with his match. [1647] (Wing M133)

PEREZ DE MONTAVLAN, JUAN. Aurora, & the Prince. [With] Oronta the Cyprian virgin: by Sig^r Girolamo Preti. Translated by T[homas] S[tanley] Esq. For H. Moseley. (Wing P1467. First edition.)

1648

BARON, ROBERT. Erotopaigeion, or the Cyprian academy. W. W., sold by J. Hardesty, T. Huntington, and T.

Jackson. (Wing B890. A re-issue of the 1647 edition.)

BERNARD, RICHARD. The isle of man. The twelfth edition. J. D. for E. Blackmore. (Wing B2026. Twelfth edition.)

DELONEY, THOMAS. The gentle craft. For J. Stafford. (Wing D953. Sixth edition.)

FAUST. The historie of the damnable life and deserved death of Doctor John Faustus. Translated by P. R. Gent. For E. Wright. (Wing H2151. Sixth edition.)

GESTA ROMANORUM. A record of ancient histories, intituled in Latine: Gesta Romanorum. R. Bishop, sold by E. Blackmore. (Wing R631. Twelfth edition.)

GOMBERVILLE, MARIN LE ROY, sieur de. The history of Polexander. Done into English by William Browne, Gent. T. Harper for T. Walkley. (Wing G1026. Second edition.)

GREENE, ROBERT. The pleasant history of Dorastus and Fawnia. For F. Faulkner. (Wing G1833. Eleventh edition.)

1649

BARON, ROBERT. An apologie for Paris, for rejecting of Juno, and Pallas, and presenting of Ate's golden ball to Venus. For T. Dring. (Wing B888)

FORDE, EMANUEL. The most famous, delectable, and pleasant history of Parismus. J. Millit, for W. Thackeray. 2v. (Wing F1532. Sixth edition. —Volume 2 printed by B. Alsop. Some copies (another edition?) have Alsop's name on both volumes [Wing F1533].)

HOWELL, JAMES. Dendrologia. Dodona's grove, or The vocall forrest. The last edition, with the addition of two other tracts. T. W. for H. Moseley. [1649] (Wing H3061. Fourth edition.)

VALENTINE AND ORSON. Valentine and Orson, The two sonnes of the Emperour of Greece. By R. Ibbitson. (Wing V28. Fifth edition.)

1650

AESOP. Aesops Fables, with their moralls, in prose and verse. R. D. for F. Eglesfield. (Wing A688. Unidentified version; the twenty-first of twenty-four editions of the fables in English during the period up to 1660.)

BAYLY, THOMAS. Herba parietis: or, The wall-flower. J. G., sold by J. Holden. (Wing B1511. First edition.)

BEAR. Beware the beare. The strange but pleasing history of Balbulo and Rosina. For E. Crowch. (Wing B2190)

BELLIANIS. The honour of chivalry: or The famous and delectable history of Don Bellianis of Greece. Translated out of Italian by L. A. B. Alsop. (Wing F781. Second edition; first edition in 1598.)

CAMUS, JEAN PIERRE. The loving enemie. Made English by Major [James] Wright. J. G., sold by J. Dakins. (Wing C415. First edition.)

CARTIGNY, JEAN DE. The voyage of the wandering knight. R. Bishop, sold by W. Gilbertson. (Wing C681. Fifth edition.)

FORDE, EMANUEL. The most pleasant historie of Ornatus and Artesia. B. A[lsop]. (Wing F1541. Fifth edition.)

FORTUNATUS. The history of the birth, travels, strange adventures, and death of Fortunatus. [1650?] (Esdaile)

FROLICKSOME, Sir HUMPHREY. The merry Oxford knight. Or, the pleasant intrigues of Sir Humphrey Frollicksome. A. M. for J. Bissel. [ca. 1650?] (Esdaile)

GARCIA, CARLOS. Lavernae, or The Spanish gipsy. Now in English by W[illiam] M[elvin]. London, not in Newgate. (Wing G212. Second edition; first edition appeared in 1638 as *The sonne of the rogue*.)

GESTA ROMANORUM. A record of ancient histories, entituled in Latine: Gesta Romanorum. R. Bishop. [1650?] (Wing R632. Thirteenth edition.) —Some copies have variant imprint: R. Bishop, sold by A. Crooke. [Wing R632A].)

HOWELL, JAMES. Dendrologia. Dodona's grove, or The vocall forrest-Second part. W. H. for H. Moseley. (Wing H3062. Part 1 first appeared in 1640.)

MAINWARINGE, M. Vienna. No art can cure this hart. For W. Leake. (Wing M295C. Fifth (?) edition of this re-working of the old romance of *Paris and Vienne*.)

MANDEVILLE, Sir JOHN. The voyages and travailes of Sir John Mandevile knight. R. B. for E. Dod and N. Ekins. (Wing M412. Twelfth edition.)

PEREZ DE MONTALVAN, JUAN. Aurora: Ismenia and the Prince. [With] Oronta the Cyprian virgin: by Sigr Girolamo Preti. Translated by Thomas Stanley. The second edition, with additions. W. Wilson for H. Moseley. (Wing P1468. Second edition.)

REYNARD THE FOX. The most delectable history of Reynard the Fox. J. Bell. (Esdaile; Harvard University Library. Eleventh edition.)

REYNOLDS, JOHN. The flower of fidelitie. T. M. and A. C. for G. Badger. (Wing R1304. First edition.)

SHEPPARD, SAMUEL. The loves of Amandus and Sophronia. G. D. for J. Hardestie. (Wing S3167)

1651

AESOP. Aesops Fables, with their moralls, in prose and verse. R. D. for F. Eglesfield. (Wing A690. Second edition of this unidentified version, of which the first edition appeared in 1650; the twenty-second of twenty-four editions of the fables in English during the period up to 1660.)

ASSARINO, LUCA. La Stratonica; or The unfortunate queen. Written in Italian and now Englished by J. B. Gent. J. Field. (Wing A4016. —Some copies have imprint: J. F. for H. Moseley.)

BACON, Sir FRANCIS. New Atlantis. In: Sylva sylvarum. The sixth edition. J. F. for W. Lee. Wing B327. Sixth edition.)

BOYLE, ROGER, Earl of Orrery. Parthenissa. [Waterford: P. de Pienne.] (Wing O488. First edition. —Contains Part 1, books 1-8 and Part 2, books 1-8.)

CHARLETON, WALTER. The Ephesian and Cimmerian matrons. [1651?] (Esdaile; First edition. —The Ephesian matron is based on Petronius; the Cimmerian matron on Puteanus.)

FIDGE, GEORGE. Hind's ramble, or, The description of his manner and course of life. For G. Latham. (Wing F854)

HIND, JAMES. The pleasant and delightful history of Captain Hind. For G. Horton. (Wing P2529A.)

QUINTANA, FRANCISCO DE. The history of Don Fenise. Written in Spanish by Francisco de las Coveras [pseud.] And now Englished by a person of Honour. For H. Moseley. (Wing Q220)

WEAMYS, ANNE. A continuation of Sir Philip Sydney's Arcadia. W. Bentley, sold by T. Heath. (Wing W1189)

1652

AMADIS DE GAULE. The famous and renowned history of Amadis de Gaule. Being the sixth part. Translated out of French into English, by Francis Kirkman. J. Bell. (Wing F358. First appearances of this part; see entries for 1618, 1619.)

AUDIGUIER, HENRI VITAL D'. A tragi-comicall history of our times, under the borrowed names of Lisander and Calista. For R. Lownes. (Wing A4194. Fourth edition.)

BALDWIN, WILLIAM. A marvellous history, entitled Beware the cat. For J. Bell. (Wing B546. Fourth edition; earlier editions in 1561, 1570, 1584.)

CAMUS, JEAN PIERRE. Nature's paradox: or, The innocent impostor. Now English'd by Major [James] Wright. J. G. for E. Dod and N. Ekins. (Wing C417)

CARMENI, FRANCESCO. Nis s e n a, an excellent new romance. Now Englished by an honorable anti-Socordist. For H. Moseley. (Esdaile. —Some copies are dated 1653.)

CERVANTES SAAVEDRA, MIGUEL DE. The history of the valorous and witty knight-errant, Don-Quixote of the Mancha. R. Hodgkinsonne, for A. Crooke. (Wing C1776. Third edition of Shelton's translation.)

CHOICE NOVELS. Choice novels, and amorous tales, written by the most refined wits of Italy. Newly translated into English. T. N. for H. Moseley. (Wing C3917)

CLERIO AND LOZIA. The loves and adventures of Clerio and Lozia. Written originally in French and translated into English. By Fra. Kirkman, Gent. J. M., sold by W. Ley. (Wing L3260. First edition.)

CODRINGTON, R O B E R T. The troublesome and hard adventures in love. Written in Spanish by Michael Cervantes; and exactly translated into English, by R[obert] C[odrington] Gent. B. Alsop. (Wing C1781. —Not by Cervantes, though translated from the Spanish.)

DELONEY, THOMAS. The gentle craft. For J. Stafford. (Wing D954. Seventh edition.)

FIDGE, GEORGE. The English Gusman; or, The history of that unparallel'd thief James Hind. T. N. for G. Latham jr. (Wing F852. First edition.)

FIDGE, GEORGE. Wit for money. For T. Vere and W. Gilbertson. [1652?] (Wing F855. —An abridgement of the preceding entry.)

LA CALPRENEDE, GAUTIER DE COSTES, sieur de. Cassandra. The fam'd romance. Now elegantly rendered into English by an honourable person [i.e. George Digby]. For H. Moseley. (Esdaile. —An octavo of 232p. containing the first three books of Part 1.)

LA CALPRENEDE, GAUTIER DE COSTES, sieur de. Cassandra. The

fam'd romance. Translated by a person of quality [i.e. Sir Charles Cotterell.] For H. Moseley. (Wing L106. —Folio; first edition of the complete translation.)

LA CALPRENEDE, GAUTIER DE COSTES, sieur de. Cleopatra. A new romance . . . now Englished by a Gent. of the Inner Temple. H. Moseley and J. Holden. (University of Illinois. —Not Loveday's translation.)

LA CALPRENEDE, GAUTIER DE COSTES, sieur de. Hymen's praeludia: or, Love's master-piece. Being the first part of Cleopatra. Now rendred into English by R. Loveday. For G. Thompson. (Wing L111. First edition of first part.)

PHILOXYPES AND POLYCRITE. The history of Philoxypes and Polycrite. Englished out of French, by an honorable anti-Socordist. For H. Moseley. (Wing H2130)

SCUDERY, MADELEINE DE. Ibrahim. Or the Illustrious Bassa. Englished by Henry Cogan Gent. For H. Moseley, W. Bentley, and T. Heath. (Wing S2160. First edition.)

1653

CARMENI, FRANCESCO. Nissena, an excellent new romance. Now Englished by an honorable anti-Socordist. For H. Moseley. (Wing C599. —Some copies are dated 1652.)

CESPEDES Y MENESES, GONZALO. Gerardo the unfortunate Spaniard. Originally in Spanish, and made English by L[eonard] D[igges]. W. Bentley, sold W. Shears. (Wing C1783. Second edition.)

CLORIA. Cloria and Narcissus. Written by an honourable person. S. G., and are to be sold by A. Williamson.

(Wing C4725. —Volume 1 only; for volume 2 see 1654.)

LAZARILLO DE TORMES. Lazarillo, or The excellent history of Lazarillo de Tormes. For W. Leake. (Wing L761. Sixth edition.)

PALMENDOS. The famous history of Palmendos, son to the most renowned Palmerin d'Oliva. Translated by A[nthony] M[unday]. E. Alsop. (Wing F377. Second edition; first edition in 1589.)

RABELAIS, FRANÇOIS. The first [-second] book of the Works of Mr. Francis Rabelais. Now faithfully translated into English [by Sir Thomas Urquhart]. For R. Baddeley. (Wing R105, R108. First edition.)

SEVEN SAGES. The history of the seven wise maisters of Rome. J. C. for E. Blackmore. (Wing H2180. Sixth edition.)

SCUDERY, MADELEINE DE. Artamenes or The grand Cyrus. Now Englished by F. G. Gent. For H. Moseley and T. Dring. (Wing S2144. First edition [parts 1-2 only].)

SOREL, CHARLES. The extravagant shepherd. The anti-romance. Translated out of French [by John Davies]. For T. Heath. (Wing S4703. First edition.)

1654

BOYLE, ROGER, Earl of Orrery. Parthenissa. For R. Lownes. (Wing O489. Second edition. —Contains Part 1, books 1-6.)

CERIZIERS, RENE DE. The innocent lady, or The illustrious innocence. Now rendered into English by Sir William Lower. T. Mabb, for W. Lee, (Wing C1679)

CERVANTES SAAVEDRA, MIGUEL DE. Delight in severall shapes. For W. Sheares. (Wing C1770. Second edition, under a new title, of James Mabbe's translation of the *Exemplary novels*.)

CLORIA. Cloria and Narcissus continued. Written by an honourable person. S. G., and are to be sold by A. Williamson. (Wing C4726. —Volume 2 only; for volume 1 see 1653.)

LA CALPRENEDE, GAUTIER DE COSTES, sieur de. Hymen's praeludia: or, Love's master-piece. Being the first part of Cleopatra. Translated by R. Loveday. J. G. for R. Lowndes. (Wing L112. Second edition.)

LA CALPRENEDE, GAUTIER DE COSTES, sieur de. Hymen's praeludia: or, Love's master-piece. The second part. Translated by R. Loveday. J. G. for R. Lowndes. (Wing L113. First edition of this part.)

LOREDANO, GIOVANNI FRANCESCO. Dianea: an excellent new romance. Translated into English by Sir Aston Cokaine. For H. Moseley. (Wing L3066)

MARGUERITE DE NAVARRE. Heptameron, or The history of the fortunate lovers. Now made English by Robert Codrington. F. L. for N. Ekins. (Wing M593. First appearance of this translation.)

REYNARD THE FOX. The most delectable history of Reynard the Fox. J. Bell. (Wing S3509. Twelfth edition.)

REYNOLDS, JOHN. The flower of fidelitie. T. Mabb, for G. Badger. (Wing R1305. Second edition.)

SCUDERY, MADELEINE DE. Artamenes or The grand Cyrus. Now Englished by F. G. Gent. For H. Moseley

and T. Dring. (Wing S2144. First edition [parts 3-4 only].)

SCUDERY, MADELEINE DE. The third volume of Artamenes or The grand Cyrus. Now Englished by F. G. Gent. For H. Moseley and T. Dring. (Wing S2162. First edition [parts 5-6 only].)

SOREL, CHARLES. The extravagant shepherd. An anti-romance. Now made English [by John Davies]. T. Newcomb for T. Heath. (Wing S4704. Second edition.)

TRIANA. Triana, or A threefold romanza of Mariana Paduana Sabina. For J. Stafford. (Wing F2470. —The ascription to Thomas Fuller is probably erroneous. First edition.)

1655

ALEMAN, MATEO. The rogue: or, The excellencie of history displayed. Epitomiz'd into English, by A. S. Gent. J. C. for the author, sold by T. Johnson and S. Chatfield. (Wing A903. First appearance of this abridgement.)

ALEMAN, MATEO. The rogue, or The second part of the life of Guzman de Alfarache. H. Hills. (Wing A904A. Volume 2 of the fifth (1656) edition.)

BIONDI, GIOVANNI FRANCESCO. Coralbo. A new romance. Now faithfully render'd into English [by R. G.]. For H. Moseley. (Wing B2935)

BOCCACCIO, GIOVANNI. The Decameron . . . The last five days. E. Cotes. (Wing B3379. Volume 2 of the fourth edition; volume 1 dated 1657.)

BOYLE, ROGER, Earl of Orrery. Parthenissa. The first part. For H. Herringman. (Wing O491. Second issue of first edition. —Contains Part 1, books 1-4. —Some copies have variant imprint: For H. Moseley [Wing O491A].)

BOYLE, ROGER, Earl of Orrery. Parthenissa. The second part. For H. Herringman. (Wing O492. Second issue of first edition. —Contains Part 1, books 5-8. —Some copies have variant imprint: For H. Moseley [Wing O492A].)

BOYLE, ROGER, Earl of Orrery. Parthenissa. The third part. For H. Herringman. (Wing O492C. Second issue of first edition. —Contains Part 2, books 1-4. —Some copies have variant imprint: For H. Moseley [Wing O492B].)

BOYLE, ROGER, Earl of Orrery. Parthenissa. The fourth part. For H. Herringman. (Wing O492D. Second issue of first edition. —Contains Part 2, books 5-8.)

CAMUS, JEAN PIERRE. Elise, or Innocencie guilty. Translated into English by Jo: Jennings, Gent. T. Newcomb for H. Moseley. (Wing C413)

CERIZIERS, RENE DE. The innocent lord: or, The divine providence. Being the incomparable history of Joseph. Now rendred into English by Sir William Lowre. S. G. for C. Adams. (Wing C1681)

CLERIO AND LOZIA. The loves and adventures of Clerio and Lozia. Written originally in French, and translated into English. By Fra. Kirkman, Gent. (Cited by Esdaile, without imprint, from Hazlitt. Second edition.)

CROUCH, HUMPHREY. A new and pleasant history of unfortunate Hodg of the South. For T. Locke. (Wing C7286)

DELONEY, THOMAS. The pleasant history of John Winchcomb, in his younger years called Jack of Newbery. (Cited by Esdaile, without imprint, from Hazlitt. Thirteenth edition.)

GREENE. ROBERT. The pleasant history of Dorastus and Fawnia. For E. Blackmore. (Wing G1834. Twelfth edition.)

JOHNSON, RICHARD. The most pleasant history of Tom a Lincoln. The ninth impression. T. R. and E. M. for F. Coles. (Wing J807. Ninth edition; no eighth edition known.)

LA CALPRENEDE, GAUTIER DE COSTES, sieur de. Hymen's praeludia: or, Love's master-piece. The third part. Translated by R. Loveday. J. G. for R. Lowndes. (Wing L114. First edition of this part.)

LAZARILLO DE TORMES. Lazarillo, or The excellent history of Lazarillo de Tormes. R. Hodgkinsonne. (Esdaile. Seventh edition.)

PRICE, LAURENCE. The witch of the woodlands. For J. Stafford. (Wing P3391. First edition.)

REYNOLDS, JOHN. The flower of fidelitie. T. Mabb, for G. Badger. (Wing R1306. Third edition.)

SCUDERY, MADELEINE DE. The fourth volume of Artamenes or The grand Cyrus. Now Englished by F. G. Gent. For H. Moseley and T. Dring. (Wing S2144. First edition [parts 7-8 only].)

SCUDERY, MADELEINE DE. The fifth and last volume of Artamenes or The grand Cyrus. Now Englished by F. G. Gent. For H. Moseley and T. Dring. (Wing S2144. First edition [parts 9-10 only].)

SCUDERY, MADELEINE DE. Clelia. An excellent new romance. [Translated by John Davies.] Volume I. For H. Moseley and T. Dring. (Wing S2151. First edition of this volume.)

SIDNEY, Sir PHILIP. The Countess of Pembroke's Arcadia. The tenth edition. W. Du Gard, sold by G. Calvert and T. Pierrepont. (Wing S3768. Fourteenth edition.)

SOREL, CHARLES. The comical history of Francion. Done into English by a person of honour. For F. Leach, sold by R. Lowndes. (Wing S4702. First edition.)

THEOPHANIA. Theophania: or Severall modern histories represented by way of romance. By an English person of quality. T. Newcomb for T. Heath. (Wing S371. Attributed to Sir W. Sales.)

1656

ALEMAN, MATEO. The rogue, or The life of Guzman de Alfarache. The fourth edition corrected. W. B. for P. Chetwind. (Wing A903A. Fourth edition.)

ALEMAN, MATEO. The rogue: or The life of Guzman de Alfarache. The fifth and last edition, corrected. J. C. for P. Chetwind, sold by T. Johnson. (Esdaile. Fifth edition. —Some copies have imprint: . . . sold by J. Hirons (Wing A904). —Volume 2 of this edition appeared in 1655.)

BOVINIAN. The most pleasant history of Bovinian. Being an addition to that most delightfull history of Crispine and Crispianus. For J. Stafford. (Wing M2914. —The history of Crispine and Crispianus forms part of Deloney's Gentle craft.)

BOYLE, ROGER, Earl of Orrery. Parthenissa. The fifth part. By T. R. and E. M. for H. Herringman. (Wing O493. First edition. —Contains Part 3, books 1-4.)

C., W. The first [-second] part of Fragosa King of Aragon. By E. Alsop. (Wing C166. Third edition.)

CAVENDISH, MARGARET, Duchess of Newcastle. Natures pictures drawn by fancies pencil to the life. In this volume there are several feigned stories. For J. Martin and J. Allestrye. (Wing N855. First edition.)

CAWWOOD THE ROOK. The pleasant history of Cawwood the Rooke. R. J. for F. Grove. (Wing P2548. Second edition.)

CERIZIERS, RENE DE. The triumphant lady; or, The crowned innocence. For G. Bedell and T. Collins. (Wing C1682)

HARRINGTON, JAMES. The common-wealth of Oceana. J. Streater, for L. Chapman. (Wing H809. One of two editions the same year; see next entry.)

HARRINGTON, JAMES. The comwealth of Oceana. For D. Pakeman. (Wing H809A)

HEYWOOD, THOMAS. The famous and remarkable history of Sir Richard Whittington. Written by T.H. W. Wilson, sold by F. Coles. (Wing H1780. First edition.)

HOLLAND, SAMUEL. Don Zara del Fogo: a mock-romance. T. W. for T. Vere. (Wing H2437. First edition.)

HOLLAND, SAMUEL. Wit and fancy in a maze. A mock-romance. T. W. for T. Vere. (Wing H2445. Another issue of the preceding entry.)

LA CALPRENEDE, GAUTIER DE COSTES, sieur de. Hymen's praeludia: or, Love's master-piece. The fourth part . . . rendred into English by J. C. For J. G. and R. Lowndes. (Wing L115. First edition of this part.)

LA CALPRENEDE, GAUTIER DE COSTES, sieur de. Hymen's praeludia: or, Love's master-piece. The fifth part . . . rendred into English by J. C. For J. G. and R. Lowndes. 1650 [i.e. 1656]. (Wing L116. First edition of this part.)

PEREZ DE MONTALVAN, JUAN. The illustrious shepherdess. The imperious brother. Now made English by E. P[hillips]. J. C. for N. Brook. (Wing P1469)

REYNARD THE FOX. The most delectable history of Reynard the Fox. J. Bell. (Wing S3510. Thirteenth edition.)

SCUDERY, MADELEINE DE. Clelia. An excellent new romance. [Translated by John Davies.] Volume II. For H. Moseley and T. Dring. (Wing S2152. First edition of this volume.)

S., E. The witty rogue . . . or, The history of . . . Richard Hainam. For E. S. (Wing S20. Chapin Library.)

1657

AESOP. Aesop's Fables, English and Latine. By W. Wilson. (Wing A691. Unidentified version; the twenty-third of twenty-four editions of the fables in English during the period up to 1660.)

BOCCACCIO, GIOVANNI. Boccace's Tales. The fourth edition. E. Cotes. (Wing B3379. Fourth edition. —Each volume has separate title: v.1, *The modell of wit, mirth, eloquence, and conversation*; v.2, *The Decameron . . . The last five days.* Title-page to v.2 dated 1655.)

BOISROBERT, FRANCOIS LE METEL DE. The Indian history of Anaxander and Orazia. Translated into English by W. G. S. G. for J. Kirton. (Wing B3468. Second edition; first edition in 1639.)

FORDE, EMANUEL. The most famous, delectable, and pleasant history of Parismus. The fifth impression. B. Alsop, for J. Andrews. (Esdaile; Quaritch 680:177. Eighth edition.)

GARCIA, CARLOS. Guzman, Hinde, and Hannam outstript. Printed, 1657. (Wing G211. Third edition; first edition in 1638 as *The sonne of the rogue.*)

GODWIN, FRANCIS. The man in the moone. To which is now added Nuncius inanimatus. Englished [from the Latin] by a person of worth. For J. Kirton. (Wing G970. Second edition.)

LA CALPRENEDE, GAUTIER DE COSTES, sieur de. Hymen's Praeludia: or, Love's masterpiece, being the first part of . . . Cleopatra. By F. L. for R. Lowndes. (Third edition of this part. —Muirhead 6:294.)

LONGUS. Daphnis and Chloe. A most sweet, and pleasant pastorall romance for young ladies. By Geo. Thornley, Gent. For J. Garfield. (Wing L3003. First appearance of this translation; a partial translation had appeared in 1587, done by Angell Daye.)

M., T. The life of a satyricall puppy called Nim. For H. Moseley. (Wing M1411. —Incorrectly ascribed to Thomas May.)

MANDEVILLE, Sir JOHN. The voyages and travels of Sir John Mandevile knight. R. B., sold by A. Crooke. (Wing M413. Thirteenth edition. —Esdaile also lists another edition, the 14th, without date.)

PEELE, GEORGE. The merrie conceited jests of George Peele. For W. Gilbertson. (Wing P1053. Fifth edition.)

QUEVEDO Y VILLEGAS, FRANCISCO DE. The life and adventures of Buscon the witty Spaniard. Put into English by a person of honour. J. M. for H. Herringman. (Wing Q190. First edition.)

REYNOLDS, JOHN. The triumphs of Gods revenge. The third edition. S. Griffin, for W. Lee. (Wing R1309. Sixth edition. —Books 2-6 have separate title-pages, dated 1656.)

SOREL, CHARLES. The extravagant shepherd. An anti-romance. T. Newcomb for T. Heath. (Wing S4700. Third edition.)

URFE, HONORE D'. Astrea. Translated by a person of quality [i.e. John Speed?]. Volume I [-II]. W. W. for H. Moseley, T. Dring, and H. Herringman. (Wing U132. First complete translation; a translation by another hand of part 1 appeared in 1620. —For v.3 of the present translation, see 1658.)

1658

AESOP. The fables of Esope. J. Owsley and P. Lillicrap, for A. Roper. (Wing A692. Caxton's version; the last of twenty-four editions of the fables in English during the period up to 1660.)

BACON, Sir FRANCIS. New Atlantis. (In: Sylva sylvarum. The seventh edition. A. M. for W. Lee, sold by T. Johnson. Wing B329. Seventh edition. —Another issue, same year, has imprint: For W. Lee, sold by T. Williams and W. Place. [Wing B328].)

BERNARD, RICHARD. The isle of man. The thirteenth edition. R. I. for E. Blackmore. (Wing B2026A. Thirteenth edition.)

HARRINGTON, JAMES. The commonwealth of Oceana. For D. Pakeman. (Wing H810. Third edition.)

LA CALPRENEDE, GAUTIER DE COSTES, sieur de. Hymen's praeludia: or, Love's master-piece. The sixth part . . . rendred into English by J[ohn] C[oles]. F. Leach, for R. Lowndes. (Wing L116A. First edition of this part.)

LA CALPRENEDE, GAUTIER DE COSTES, sieur de. Hymen's praeludia: or, Love's master-piece. The seventh part . . . rendred into English by J[ohn] C[oles]. For H. Moseley and J. Crook. (Wing L117. First edition of this part. —Another issue same year has imprint: For H. Moseley. [Wing L117A].)

LA CALPRENEDE, GAUTIER DE COSTES, sieur de. Hymen's praeludia: or, Love's master-piece. The eighth part . . . rendred into English by J[ames] W[ebb]. For H. Moseley. (Wing L118. First edition of this part.)

LA CALPRENEDE, GAUTIER DE COSTES, sieur de. Hymen's praeludia: or, Love's master-piece. The ninth [and tenth] part . . . rendred in English by J[ohn] D[avies]. E. Tyler, for J. Crook. (University of Virginia Library. —First edition of these parts.)

SCUDERY, MADELEINE DE. Clelia. An excellent new romance. [Translated by John Davies.] Volume III. For H. Moseley and T. Dring. (Wing S2153. First edition of this volume.)

URFE, HONORE D'. Astrea. Translated by a person of quality [i.e. John Speed?]. Volume III. W. W. for H. Moseley, T. Dring, and H. Herringman. (Wing U132)

1659

BACON, Sir FRANCIS. New Atlantis. A work unfinished. T. Newcomb. (Wing B308. Eighth (first separate) edition; issued as a supplement to *Mr. Bushell's Abridgement of Bacon's Philosophical Theory.*)

BERNARD, RICHARD. The isle of man. The thirteenth edition. For N. Ranew. (Wing B2027. Fourteenth edition.)

BRATHWAIT, RICHARD, supposed author. Panthalia: or The royal romance. J. G., sold by A. Williamson. (Wing B4273. —Signed: Castalion Pomerano.)

CHARLETON, WALTER. The Ephesian matron. For H. Herringman. (Wing C3671. Second edition.)

CYRANO DE BERGERAC, HERCULE SAVINIEN DE. Selenarchia, or The government of the world in the moon. Done into English by Tho. St Serf, Gent. J. Cottrel, sold by H. Robinson. (Wing C7719)

LA CALPRENEDE, GAUTIER DE COSTES, sieur de. Hymen's praeludia: or, Love's master-piece. The ninth and tenth part . . . rendred into English by J[ohn] D[avies]. For H. Moseley and J. Crook. (Wing L119. Second edition of these parts.)

LA CALPRENEDE, GAUTIER DE COSTES, sieur de. Hymen's praeludia: or, Love's master-piece. The elev-

enth, twelfth, and last parts . . . rendred into English by J[ohn] D[avies]. For H. Moseley. (Wing L120. First edition of these parts.)

LOREDANO, GIOVANNI FRANCESCO. The life of Adam. Now rendered into English by J. S. For H. Moseley. (Wing L3067)

RUSH, FRIAR. The historie of Frier Rush. J. Bell. (Wing H2121. Fourth edition.)

1660

BACON, Sir FRANCIS. New Atlantis. Continued by R.H. For J. Crooke. (Wing B309. Ninth edition.)

BRUSONI, GIROLAMO. Arnaldo, or, The injur'd lover. Made English by T. S. For T. Dring. (Wing B5241)

CRISPE, SAMUEL. Don Samuel Crispe: or, The pleasant history of the Knight of Fond Love. [For H. Marsh, 1660.] (Wing D1846)

DELONEY, THOMAS. The honour of the gentle craft. The last and best part. G. P. for I. Andrews. (Wing D954A. Eighth edition.)

FORDE, EMANUEL. The pleasant history of Parismus prince of Bohemia.. J. B. for C. Tyus. (Esdaile. Undated abridgement of 24p.)

GEORGE, Saint. The life and death of the famous champion of England, St. George. For F. Coles, T. Vere, and W. Gilbertson. [1660] (Wing L2015. First edition.)

HOLLAND, SAMUEL. Romanciomastrix, or A romance on romances. For the author. (Wing H2443. Second edition; first edition in 1656 as *Don Zara del Fogo.*)

INGELO, NATHANIEL. Bentivolio and Urania. J. G. for R. Marriot. (Wing I175. First edition. —Esdaile lists a second issue the same year.)

JOHNSON, RICHARD. The famous history of the seven champions of Christendom. J. B. for A. Crook [1660]. (Wing J796. Seventh edition. —Volume 2 (Wing J801) has imprint: G. Dawson for A. Crook.)

MACKENZIE, Sir GEORGE. Aretina: or, The serious romance. Part first. Edinburgh: For R. Broun. (Wing M151. First edition.)

ORTIGUE, PIERRE D', sieur de Vaumoriere. The grand Scipio, an excellent new romance. Rendered into English by G. H. For H. Mosely, T. Dring, and H. Herringman. (Wing V162)

PRACTICAL PART OF LOVE. The practical part of love. Extracted out of the extravagant and lascivious life of a fair but subtle female. (Wing P3154)

REYNOLDS, JOHN. The flower of fidelitie. For R. Horne. (Wing R1307. Fourth edition.)

SCUDERY, MADELEINE DE. Clelia. An excellent new romance. [Translated by George Havers.] Volume IV. For H. Moseley and T. Dring. (Wing S2154. First edition of this volume.)

SOREL, CHARLES. The extravagant shepherd. An anti-romance. Published the second time. For T. Bassett. (Wing S4701. Fourth edition.)

ALEMAN, MATEO. Guzman de Alfarache. The fifth edition. H. Marsh. [1661?] (Cited by Esdaile from Marsh's list; no copy known. Sixth edition.)

BURTON, JOHN. The history of Eriander. The first part. R. Davenport for J. Williams. (Wing B6180)

C., S. The famous and delectable history of Cleocreton & Cloryana. J. B. for C. Tyus. (STC 4302. Undated; although the STC dates the book [1630?] it is likely that a date of ca. 1660 is more nearly correct.)

CARTIGNY, JEAN DE. The voyage of the wandring knight. Translated out of French into English by W[illiam] G[oodyear]. J. Cadwell for A. Crooke. (Wing C681A. Sixth edition.)

CLORIA. The Princess Cloria: or, The royal romance. Written by a person of honour. R. Wood, sold by W. Brooke. (Wing P3492. First complete edition; parts appeared earlier in 1653-54.)

DAUNCEY, JOHN. The English lovers: a romance. The second part. (First part and general title-page dated 1662.)

ELIANA. Eliana. A new romance: formed by an English hand. T. R. for P. Dring. (Wing E499)

FORDE, EMANUEL. The famous history of Montelyon. By E. Alsop, and R. Wood, sold by F. Grove, W. Gilbertson, and C. Tyus. (Wing F1523. Third known edition.)

FORDE, EMANUEL. The most famous, delectable, and pleasant history of Parismus. The sixth impression. By E. Alsop, for F. Grove, and W. G i l b e r t s o n. (Wing F1533A. Ninth edition.)

FRIAR BACON. The famous history of Fryer Bacon. E. Cotes for F. Grove. (Wing F371. Fifth edition.)

GUY OF WARWICK. The famous history of Guy of Warwick. By Samuel Smithson. For F. Coles, T. Vere, J. Wright, and J. Clarke. [ca.1661] (Wing F376. First edition of this version.)

JOHNSON, RICHARD. The most illustrious history of the seven champions of Christendome. For W. Gilbertson. (Q u a r i t c h 676:241. An abridgement.)

LA CALPRENEDE, GAUTIER DE COSTES, sieur de. Cassandra: the fam'd romance. Now elegantly rendred into English. By Sir Charles Cotterell. For H. Moseley. (Wing L107. Second edition.)

MACKENZIE, Sir GEORGE. Aretina: or, The serious romance. Part first. For R. Smith. (Wing M152. Reissue of the 1660 edition. —Another reissue of perhaps the same year has imprint: For G. S[awbridge], with no imprint date. Wing M153.)

M O N T E L I O N, pseud. Don Juan Lamberto: or, A commical history of the late times. The first part. J. Brudenell, for H. Marsh. (Clark Library, UCLA. First edition. —Sometimes attributed to Thomas Flatman or John Phillips.)

M O N T E L I O N, pseud. Don Juan Lamberto: or, A comical history of the late times. The first [-second] part[s]. By Montelion Knight of the Oracle, &c. Sold by H. Marsh. (Wing M2491 (pt.1). —Pt.2 has imprint: T. Leach, for H. Marsh.)

MONTELION, pseud. Don Juan Lamberto, or A comical history of the late times. By Montelion, Knight of the Oracle, &c. The second edition corrected. J. Brudenell for H. Marsh. 2v. (Wing M2492. Second edition.)

ORTIGUE, PIERRE D', sieur de Vaumoriere. The second volume of the Grand Scipio. Rendred into English by G[eorge] H[avers]. For T. Dring. (Wing V162A. First appearance of this part; parts 1 and 2 had appeared in 1660.)

REYNOLDS, JOHN. Blood for blood: or Murthers revenged. In thirty tragical histories. To which are added five more. By T[homas] M[anley] Esq. Oxford: For the author. (Wing R1303. A pirated abridgement of Reynolds' *Triumphs of Gods revenge*.)

ROBERTS, HENRY. The famous history of Pheander the Maiden Knight. For T. Fawcet, sold by F. Coles. (Wing R1597A. Fifth edition.)

SALTON, W., pseud.? [Somnia allegorica: or Dreams expounded. A novel. The second edition.] (Cited by Esdaile, without imprint, from Anthony a Wood.)

SCUDERY, MADELEINE DE. Clelia. An excellent new romance. [Translated by George Havers.] Volume V. For H. Moseley and T. Dring. (Wing S2155. First edition of this volume.)

SOREL, CHARLES. The most de- S3511. Fourteenth edition.)

REYNOLDS, JOHN. The triumphs of Gods revenge. For W. Lee. (Wing R1310. Seventh edition.)
lightfull and pleasant history of Francion. Done into English by a person of honour. For S. Miller. (Wing S4704B)

DAUNCEY, JOHN. The English lovers: or A girle worth gold. Both parts . . . newly formed into a romance. By . . . I[ohn] D[auncey] Gent. For F. Kirkman and H. Marsh. (Folger Library. Part 2 has also separate title-page dated 1661. —Also issued with cancel title having imprint: For H. Browne. (Wing D289A) —A prose version of Heywood's *The fair maid of the west.*)

FORDE, EMANUEL. The most pleasant historie of Ornatus and Artesia. By E. Alsop and R. Wood, for T. Vere and W. Gilbertson. (Wing F1541A. Sixth edition.)

GESTA ROMANORUM. A record of ancient histories, intituled in Latine: Gesta Romanorum. J. B. for A. Crook. (Wing R633. Fourteenth edition.)

LA CALPRENEDE, GAUTIER DE COSTES, sieur de. Pharamond: or, The history of France. A new romance. Now elegantly rendred into English [by John Davies]. J. Cottrell for N. Brook and S. Speed. (Wing L125. First edition.)

REYNARD THE FOX. The most delectable history of Reynard the Fox. By H. B., sold by E. Brewster. (Wing

ROBIN HOOD. The noble birth and gallant atchievements of . . . Robin Hood. For T. Vere and W. Gilbertson. (Wing N1201. First edition.)

SIDNEY, Sir PHILIP. The Countess of Pembroke's Arcadia. The eleventh edition. H. Lloyd for W. Du-Gard, sold by G. Calvert and T. Pierrepont. (Wing S3769. Fifteenth edition.)

1663

BELLIANIS. The honour of chivalry. Or the famous and delectable history of Don Bellianis of Greece. E. A. and T. F. for F. Coles, W. Gilbertson, and C. Tyus. (University of Illinois Library. Third edition.)

BIONDI, GIOVANNI FRANCESCO. Donzella desterrada, or, The banish'd virgin. Englished by I[ames] H[ayward]. For A. Moseley. [1663?] (Cited by Esdaile from Anne Moseley's list. Second edition.)

BLONDO, GIUSEPPE. The penitent bandito: or The history of the conversion & death of the most illustrious lord signor Troilo Sauelli. The second edition. By Sir T[obie] M[atthew] Knight. (Wing P1232. No first edition known)

C., W. The history of the most renowned Fragosa King of Aragon. E. Alsop and R. Wood. 2v. (Wing C155. Fourth edition.)

FIREDRAKE. The knight-adventurer: or, The infamous and abominable history of . . . Sir Firedrake. R. J. (Wing K697)

FORDE, EMANUEL. The famous history of Montelyon. E. Alsop and R. Wood for S. S., sold by F. Coles and C. Tyus. (Wing F1524. Fourth known edition.)

FORDE, EMANUEL. The most famous, delectable, and pleasant history of Parismus. E. Alsop and R. Wood for S. S., sold by F. Coles. (Esdaile. Tenth edition.)

GESTA ROMANORUM. A record of ancient histories, intituled in Latine: Gesta Romanorum. J. B. for A. Crook. (Wing R634. Fifteenth edition.)

GRISELDA. The true and admirable history of Patient Grisel. For Eliz. Andrews. (Wing T2411. Third edition.)

HOWARD, THOMAS. The history of the seven wise mistresses of Rome. For M. Wright. (Wing H3008. First edition.)

LA CALPRENEDE, GAUTIER DE COSTES, sieur de. Hymen's Praeludia: or, Love's master-piece. The first [-third] part[s]. Rendred into English by R. Loveday. R. D. for R. Lownds. (Wing L121. Second edition of these parts.)

LA CALPRENEDE, GAUTIER DE COSTES, sieur de. Hymen's Praeludia: or, Love's master-piece. Being the six last parts . . . rendred into English by J. C[oles] and J. D[avies]. E. M. for A. Moseley. (Part of Wing L122. Second edition of these parts. —Parts 9-10 have separate title-page with imprint: For H. Moseley and J. Crook, 1659; parts 11-12: For H. Moseley, 1659.)

LEFEVRE, RAOUL. The destruction of Troy. The seventh edition. R. I. for S. S., sold by F. Coles and C. Tyus. 3 pts. (Wing L929, L934, L938. Ninth edition.)

LUCIAN. Part of Lucian made English from the originall. By Jasper Mayne. To which are adjoyned those other Dialogues of Lucian as they were formerly translated by Mr. Francis Hickes. Oxford: H. Hall, for R. Davis. (Wing L3434. First appeare of Mayne's translation. —The second part, by Hickes, has separate title-page (Wing L3425); it first appeared in 1634.)

P., J. The pleasant and delightful history of Floridon and Lucina. By J. P. T. Mabb, sold by W. Gilbertson. (Wing P64)

PALMENDOS. The famous history of Palmendos, son to the most renowned Palmerin d'Oliva. Translated by

A[nthony] M[unday]. T. Fawcet, sold by F. Coles. (Wing F378. Third edition.)

REYNOLDS, JOHN. The triumphs of Gods revenge. The fourth edition. S. Griffin, for W. Lee. (Wing R1311. Eighth edition.)

SAULNIER, GILBERT, sieur du Verdier. The love and armes of the Greeke princes. Or, The romant of romants. A. Moseley. (Cited by Esdaile, with question mark, from Anne Moseley's list. Second edition.)

1664

AMADIS DE GAULE. The fifth book of the most pleasant and delectable history of Amadis de Gaule. T. J. for A. Kembe and C. Tyus. (Wing L2731. First edition of this part. —Translated by J. Johnson?)

BACON, Sir FRANCIS. New Atlantis. (In: Sylva sylvarum. The eighth edition. J. F. and S. G. and W. Lee, sold by T. Williams. (Wing B330. Tenth edition.)

BELLIANIS. The honour of chivalry: or, The famous and delectable history of Don Bellianis of Greece. The second part. Now newly written in English by F[rancis] K[irkman]. T. Johnson, sold by A. Kembe. (Wing K633. First edition of this part.)

BULTEEL, JOHN. Birinthea, a romance. T. Mabbe for J. Playfere. (Wing B5454)

C., W. The history of the most renowned Fragosa King of Aragon. For C. Tyus. (Cited by Esdaile from an advertisement in *Palladine*, 1664. Fifth edition.)

FORDE, EMANUEL. The most famous, delectable, and pleasant history of Parismus. The seventh impression.

G. Purslowe, for F. Coles, T. Vere, W. Gilbertson, and J. Wright. (Esdaile; Princeton University Library. Part 1 only. Eleventh edition.)

GREENE, ROBERT. The pleasant history of Dorastus and Fawnia. R. Ibbitson for J. Wright, sold W. Thackery. (Wing G1835. Thirteenth edition.)

HERBERAY, NICOLAS DE. The most excellent history of . . . Don Flores of Greece. Being, a supplement to Amadis de Gaule. Translated into English by W. F. The third edition. For R. I. (Wing H1493. First known edition. —Another edition printed for A. Kembe was advertised the same year.)

INGELO, NATHANIEL. Bentivolio and Urania. The second part. J. Grismond for R. Marriott. (Wing I179. First appearance of this part (books 5-6) ; books 1-4 first appeared in 1660.)

LA CALPRENEDE, GAUTIER DE COSTES, sieur de. Cassandra the fam'd romance. Now elegantly rendred into English. By Sir Charles Cotterell. For A. Moseley. (Wing L108. Third edition.)

LUCIAN. Part of Lucian made English from the original. By Jasper Mayne. To which are adjoyned those other Dialogues of Lucian as they were formerly translated by Mr. Francis Hickes. Oxford: H. Hall for R. Davis. (Wing L3435. Second edition. —The second part, by Hickes, has separate title-page, dated 1663.)

MRS. MONEY. The death and burial of Mistress Money. E. Cotes, sold by C. Tyus. (Wing D500. First edition.)

MONTELION, pseud. Don Juan Lamberto, or A comical history of the late times. By Montelion, Knight of the Oracle. The third edition, corrected. For H. Marsh. 2v. (Wing M2492A. Third edition.)

PALLADINE. The famous, pleasant, and delightful historie, of Palladine of England. T. J. for A. Kembe and C. Tyus. (Wing C5090. Second edition; first edition appeared in 1588. —Translated by Anthony Munday.)

PALMERIN OF ENGLAND. The famous history of the noble and valiant Prince Palmerin. The first [-second] part[s]. Translated out of French by A[nthony] M[unday]. R. I. for S. S., sold by C. Tyus. 2v. (Wing H3794, H3795. Fifth edition.)

RABELAIS, FRANÇOIS. The works of the famous Mr. Francis Rabelais. Translated into English by Sr. Thomas Vrchard Kt. For R. B., sold by J. Starkey. (Wing R103. Books 1-2 only; second edition. —A reissue of the edition of 1653, with a general title-page; the special title-pages for each part are still dated 1653.)

TRIANA. Triana, or A threefold romanza of Mariana Paduana Sabina. For J. Stafford. (Wing F2471. Second edition. —Although Thomas Fuller's name appears on the title-page of this edition, the work is probably not his.)

VALENTINE AND ORSON. The famous history of Valentine and Orson, the two sons of the Emperour of Greece. For C. Tyus. (Cited by Esdaile from an advertisement in *Palladine*, 1664. Sixth edition.)

1665

CASTILLO SOLORZANO, ALONSO DE. La picara, or The triumphs of female subtilty. Rendr'd into English by John Davies of Kidwelly. W. W. for J. Starkey. (Wing C1232A)

CLORIA. The Princesse Cloria: or, The royal romance. Written by a person of honour. The second edition. For E. Man. (Wing P3493. Second complete edition.)

CROWNE, JOHN. Pandion and Amphigenia. J. G. for R. Mills. (Wing C7396)

FORDE, EMANUEL. The most famous, delectable, and pleasant history of Parismus. The second part. The seventh impression. T. Fawcet, for F. Coles, T. Vere, W. Gilbertson, and J. Wright. (Esdaile; Princeton University Library. Eleventh edition. —Part 1 of this edition appeared in 1664.)

HEAD, RICHARD. The English rogue described, in the life of Meriton Latroon. For H. Marsh. (Wing H1246. Part 1 only. First edition.)

LA CALPRENEDE, GAUTIER DE COSTES, sieur de. Hymen's Praeludia: or, Love's master-piece. R. D. for A. Moseley and J. Crooke. (Wing L122. Parts 1-6 only. Second edition of these parts.)

MONTELION, pseud. Don Juan Lambetro, or A comical history of the late times. For H. Marsh. (Cited by Esdaile from Hazlitt. Fourth edition.)

PATRICK, SIMON. The parable of the pilgrim. R. White for F. Tyton. (Wing P826. First edition.)

SCARRON, PAUL. The comical romance. Turned into English by J. B[ulteel]. J. Playfere, and W. Crooke. (Wing S830A. First edition.)

SCARRON, PAUL. Scarron's Novels. Rendred into English by John Davies of Kidwelly. For T. Dring. (Columbia University Library. —Contains four tales only. J. E. Tucker (*Rev. litt. comp.* XXIV (1950), 558-563) presents evidence to show that there

must have been a separate edition of the three other tales earlier, probably ca.1660, and that there was a second edition before 1665.)

SCARRON, PAUL. Scarron's Novels. Rendred into English by John Davies of Kidwelly. For T. Dring. (Wing S833. First complete edition of all seven tales. —Tucker (*ibid.*, p.561) lists two issues.)

1666

AESOP. Aesop's Fables, with his life. The English by Tho. Philipott Esq. W. Godbid, sold by A. Seile and E. Powell. (Wing A696. First edition of this version; the 25th of 40 editions of the fables in English during the period up to 1700. —Has also engraved title-page with date 1665 [Wing A694].)

AESOP. Aesop's Fables, with his life. The English by Tho. Philipott Esq. R. Newcomb for F. Barlow. [1666?] (Wing A695. The 26th of 40 editions of the fables in English during the period up to 1700.)

CAVENDISH, MARGARET, Duchess of Newcastle. The description of a new world, called the blazing world. A. Maxwell. (Wing N849. First edition.)

FRIAR BACON. The famous history of Fryer Bacon. E. Cotes, sold by T. Passinger. (Wing F372. Sixth edition.)

HEAD, RICHARD. The English rogue described, in the life of Meriton Latroon. For F. Kirkman. (Wing H1247. First part only. S. Gibson's bibliography of Kirkman notes three editions this year, the second, third, and fourth.)

41

LA FAYETTE, MARIE MADELEINE, comtesse de. The princess of Monpensier. (Wing L171)

1667

CAMUS, JEAN PIERRE. The loving enemie. Made English by Major [James] Wright. The second edition revised. For T. Rooks. (Wing C416. Second edition.)

CROKE, CHARLES. Fortune's uncertainty, or Youth's unconstancy. For T. Dring. (Wing C7008)

HEAD, R I C H A R D. The English rogue described, in the life of Meriton Latroon. For F. Kirkman. (Wing H1247A. First part only. Fifth edition.)

HEAD, RICHARD. The life and death of Mother Shipton. For W. Harris. (Cited by Esdaile from an [1881] reprint. First edition.)

LA CALPRENEDE, GAUTIER DE COSTES, sieur de. Cassandra, the fam'd romance. Now elegantly rendred into English. By Sir Charles Cotterell. For A. Moseley. (Wing L109. Fourth edition.)

PATRICK, SIMON. The parable of the pilgrim. R. White for F. Tyton. (Wing P827. Second edition.)

QUEVEDO Y VILLEGAS, FRANCISCO DE. Visions Made English by R[oger] L[Estrange]. For H. Herringman. (Wing Q196. First edition of this translation.)

QUEVEDO Y VILLEGAS, FRANCISCO DE. Visions. Made English by R[oger] L[Estrange]. The second edition corrected. For H. Herringman. (Wing Q196A. Second edition.)

SCARRON, PAUL. Scarron's Novels. Rendred into English by John Davies of Kidwelly. For T. Dring. (Wing S834. Second complete edition.)

1668

BERNARD, RICHARD. The isle of man. The fourteenth edition. T. Milbourn for T. S., sold by J. Wright. (Wing B2028. Fifteenth edition.)

CAVENDISH, MARGARET, Duchess of Newcastle. The description of a new world, called the blazing world. A. Maxwell. (Wing N850. Second edition.)

C H A R L E T O N, WALTER. The Ephesian and Cimmerian matrons. Two notable examples of the power of love and wit. For H. Herringman. (Wing C3670. Second edition. —Part 2 has separate title: *The Cimmerian matron, to which is added, The mysteries and miracles of love. By P. M. Gent.*) (Wing C3667)

DESJARDINS, MARIE CATHERINE HORTENSE, Mme. de Villedieu. The husband forc'd to be jealous. A translation by N. H. For H. Herringman. (Wing H3805)

FONTAINES, LOUIS, pseud. A relation of the country of Jansenia. Newly translated into English by P. B. [i.e. Peter Bellon?]. For the author, sold by A. Banks and C. Harper. (Wing F1410. —Fontaines is the pseudonym of Père Zacharie de Lisieux.)

FORDE, EMANUEL. The famous history of Montelyon. T. F. for S. S., sold by W. Thackeray. (Wing F1525. Fifth known edition.)

FORDE, EMANUEL. The most famous, delectable and pleasant history of Parismus. (Cited by Esdaile, without imprint, from Hazlitt. Part 1 only? Twelfth edition.)

GESTA ROMANORUM. A record of ancient histories, intituled in Latine: Gesta Romanorum. A. I. for A. Crook. (Wing R635. Sixteenth edition.)

HEAD, RICHARD. The English rogue described, in the life of Meriton Latroon. For F. Kirkman, sold by him and T. Dring the younger. (Wing H1248. First part only. Sixth edition.)

HEAD, RICHARD. The English rogue, continued, in the life of Meriton Latroon. The second part. For F. Kirkman. (Wing H1248A. First edition of this continuation by Kirkman.)

JOHNSON, RICHARD. The most pleasant history of Tom a Lincoln. The tenth impression. G. Purslow, for F. Coles. (Wing J810. Tenth edition.)

LA CALPRENEDE, GAUTIER DE COSTES, sieur de. Hymen's praeludia: or, Love's master-piece. R. D. for A. Moseley and J. Crooke. (Wing L122A. Third edition.)

NEVILLE, HENRY. The isle of pines. S. G. for A. Banks and C. Harper. Wing N505. —The narrative of George Pine alone.)

NEVILLE, HENRY. A new and further discovery of the islle [sic] of pines. For A. Bankes and C. Harper. (Wing N509. —The narrative of Van Sloetten alone.)

NEVILLE, HENRY. The isle of pines. For A. Banks and C. Harper. (Wing N506. —Both narratives.)

PATRICK, SIMON. The parable of the pilgrim. R. White for F. Tyton. (Wing P828. Third edition.)

QUEVEDO Y VILLEGAS, FRANCISCO DE. Visions. Made English by R[oger] L[Estrange]. The third edition corrected. For H. Herringman. (Wing Q197. Third edition.)

QUEVEDO Y VILLEGAS, FRANCICO DE. Visions. Now made English by J. Dodington, Esquire. The true edition. For J. Playfere. (Wing Q196B. —Same text as L'Estrange's translation; fourth edition.)

WINSTANLEY, WILLIAM. The honour of merchant-taylors. P. L. for W. Whitwood. (Wing W3064)

1669

BOYLE, ROGER, Earl of Orrery. Parthenissa. The last part. The sixth tome. For H. Herringman. (Wing O494. First edition of these parts. —Contains part 3, books 5-8; other parts appeared 1651-56.)

BRATHWAIT, RICHARD. The history of moderation. Written by Hesychius Pamphilus [pseud.]: and now faithfully translated out of the original. For T. Parkhurst. (Wing B4264)

DU BAIL, LOUIS MOREAU, sieur. The famous Chinois or The loves of several of the French nobility. E. O. for T. Dring. (Wing D2404. —Translator's preface signed Eleutherius.)

FORDE, EMANUEL. The most pleasant history of Ornatus and Artesia. J. W. for T. Vere, and W. Whitwood. (Wing F1542. Seventh edition.)

FORDE, EMANUEL. The most famous, delectable, and pleasant history of Parismus. (Cited by Esdaile, without imprint, from Hazlitt. Part 2 only? Twelfth edition.)

HALL, JOSEPH. Psittacorum regio. The land of parrots: or, The she-lands. For F. Kirkman. (Wing H401A and Q193. —An abridgment of Hall's *Discovery of a new world*.)

INGELO, NATHANIEL. Bentivolio and Urania. The second edition. For T. Dring, J. Starkey, and T. Basset. (Wing I1176. Second edition.)

LAZARILLO DE TORMES. Lazarillo, or The excellent history of Lazarillo de Tormes. B. G. for W. Leake. (Wing L762. Eighth edition. —Volume 1 only; v.2 appeared the following year. —The Rowland translation revised by James Blakeston.)

LETI, GREGORIO. The loves of Charles, Duke of Mantua, and of Margaret, Countess of Rovera. Translated out of the Italian. H. Herringman. (Wing L3274. First edition.)

1670

AESOP. Aesops Fables, with their moralls, in prose and verse. For F. Eglesfield. (Esdaile. Third edition of this unidentified version, of which the first appeared in 1650; the 27th of 40 editions of the fables in English during the period up to 1700.)

BACON, Sir FRANCIS. New Atlantis. (In: Sylva sylvarum. The ninth edition. J. R. for W. Lee. Wing B331. Eleventh edition. —Some copies have variant title-page with the names of the booksellers added (Gibson 179b).))

CARTIGNY, JEAN DE. The voyage of the wandring knight. Translated out of French into English by W[illiam] G[oodyear]. E. Crowch, for A. Crooke. (Wing C682. Seventh edition.)

DELONEY, THOMAS. The gentle craft. For F. Coles. [ca.1670] (Cited by Esdaile from Hazlitt. Ninth edition.)

HIND, JAMES. No jest like a true jest: being a compendious record of the merry life and mad exploits of Capt. James Hind. For T. Vere and W. Gilbertson. [1670?] (Wing N1177A. First edition.)

JOHNSON, RICHARD. The famous history of the seven champions of Christendom. G. P. for A. Crook. 2v. (Wing J797. Eighth edition. —Volume 2 (Wing J802) has imprint: E. Crowch for A. Crook.)

JOHNSON, RICHARD. The famous history of the seven champions of Christendom. R. B. for A. Crook. 2v? (Newberry Library (pt. 1 only). No date on title-page; arbitrarily dated by being placed here. Ninth edition.)

LAZARILLO DE TORMES. The pursuit of the history of Lazarillo de Tormes. B. G. for W. Leake. (Wing L762. Eighth edition. —Volume 2 only; volume 1 appeared the preceding year.)

LEFEVRE, RAOUL. The destruction of Troy. The eight edition. For T. Passenger. 3v. (Wing L930, L935, L939. Tenth edition. —Imprints to 2d and 3d parts vary slightly.)

MANDEVILLE, Sir JOHN. The voyages and travels of Sir John Mandevile knight. For A. Crooke. (Wing M414. Fifteenth edition.)

P., J. The merry conceits and passages of Simon and Cisley, two Lancashire lovers. H. B., for J. Clark, W. Thackery, and T. Passinger. [ca.1670?] (Esdaile)

PATRICK, SIMON. The parable of the pilgrim. R. White for F. Tyton. (Wing P829. Fourth edition.)

POPE, WALTER. The memoirs of Monsieur du Vall. For H. Brome. (Wing P2912)

44

PRESTON, RICHARD GRAHAM, viscount. Angliae speculum morale . . . with the Life of Theodatus, and three novels. For H. Herringman. (Wing P3310. First edition.)

QUEVEDO Y VILLEGAS, FRANCISCO DE. The life and adventures of Buscon the witty Spaniard. The second edition. For H. Herringman. (Wing Q191A. Second edition.)

REYNOLDS, JOHN. The triumphs of Gods revenge. The fifth and last edition. A. M. for W. Lee, sold by G. Sawbridg [etc.] (Wing R1312. Ninth edition. —Title-pages to Books 2 and 3 are dated 1669.)

ROSAMUND. The life and death of Rosamund. For F. Coles, T. Vere, J. Wright, J. Clarke, W. Thackeray, and T. Passinger. [ca.1670] (Wing L2009. First edition?)

SALAS BARBADILLO, A L O N S O GERONIMO. The fortunate fool. Translated into English by Philip Ayres, Gent. M. Pitt. (Wing S369)

SCARRON, PAUL. The unexpected choice, a novel. Rendred into English . . . by John Davies of Kidwelly, Gent. For J. Martyn. (Wing S837)

VILLIERS, CLAUDE DESCHAMPS, sieur de. The gentleman apothecary. Turn'd out of French. For H. Brome. (Wing V390. First edition.)

1671

A M O R O U S TRAVELLERS. The amorous travellers, or Night adventures. Written originally in Spanish . . . translated into French . . . and into English by J. B. For A. Isted and J. Edwin. (Esdaile)

BELLIANIS. The honour of chivalry: or, The famous and delectable history of Don Bellianis of Greece. Now newly written in English by F. K[irkman]. T. Johnson, for F. Kirkman. 2 pts. (Wing K633A (pt. 2). Fourth edition of part 1, second of part 2.)

BLAIR, BRYCE. The vision of Theodorus Verax. For W. Leake. (Wing B3125)

BOURSAULT, EDME. Deceptio visus: or Seeing and believing are two things. For J. Starkey. (Wing D516)

CAVENDISH, MARGARET, Duchess of Newcastle. Natures pictures drawn by fancies pencil to the life. Being several feigned stories. The second edition. A. Maxwell. (Wing N856. Second edition.)

CHAVIGNY DE LA BRETONNIERE, FRANÇOIS DE. The inconstant-lover: an excellent romance. Translated out of French. For T. Dring. (Wing C3758)

DESJARDINS, MARIE CATHERINE HORTENSE, Mme. de Villedieu. Love's journal: a romance, made of the court of Henry the II. of France. And now made English. T. Ratcliff and M. Daniel. (Wing D1189)

FORDE, EMANUEL. The famous history of Montelyon. (Cited by Esdaile, without imprint, from Hazlitt. Sixth edition.)

FORDE, EMANUEL. The most famous, delectable, and pleasant history of Parismus. The ninth impression. A. P. for F. Coles, T. Vere, and J. Wright. 2v. (Wing F1534. Thirteenth edition. — Volume 2 is sometimes dated 1672.)

FURETIERE, ANTOINE. Scarron's City romance, made English. T. N. for H. Herringman. (Wing S830)

HEAD, R I C H A R D. The English rogue. [Parts 1-4.] For F. Kirkman.

(Wing H1249 (pt.2), H1249A (pt. 3), H1250A (pt.4). First appearance of all four parts.)

MACHIAVELLI, NICCOLO. The marriage of Belphegor. (In: Quevedo's Novels. For J. Starkey. Wing Q192. Second edition.)

PANTON, EDWARD. Speculum juventutis: or, A true mirror . . . portrayed to the life in the legend of Sisaras and Vallinda. For C. Smith, and T. Burrell. (Wing P277)

PEELE, GEORGE. The merry conceited jests of George Peele. For W. Whitwood. (Wing P1054. Sixth edition.)

QUEVEDO Y VILLEGAS, FRANCISCO DE. The novels of Dom Francisco de Quevedo Villegas. Faithfully Englished. Whereunto is added, The marriage of Belphegor . . . translated from Machiavel. For J. Starkey. (Wing Q192)

QUEVEDO Y VILLEGAS, FRANCISCO DE. Visions. Made English by R[oger] L[Estrange]. The fourth edition corrected. For H. Herringman. (Wing Q198. Fifth edition.)

SCHOOTEN, HENDRIK VAN, pseud.? The hairy giants: or, A description of two islands in the South Sea. Now Englished by P. M. Gent. A. Maxwell for J. Watson, sold by J. Collins. (Wing S888)

SEVEN SAGES. The history of the seven wise masters of Rome. For J. Wright. (Wing H2181. Seventh edition.)

VALENTINE AND ORSON. Valentine and Orson, the two sons of the Emperour of Greece. G. Purslow for T. Passinger. (Wing V28A. Seventh edition.)

ANNALS OF LOVE. The annals of love, containing select histories of the amours of divers princes courts, pleasantly related. For J. Starkey. (Wing A3215)

BARLAAM AND JOASAPH. The history of the five wise philosophers. By H. P. For D. Page, T. Passenger, and B. Hurlock. (Wing P946. First edition.)

BELLIANIS. The honour of chivalry: or, The famous and delectable history of Don Bellianis of Greece. The third part. Now newly written by Fra. Kirkman. E. Okes, for F. Kirkman. (Esdaile; Wing lists as K634 a 1682 edition, possibly in error for this of 1672. —First appearance of this part; parts 1 and 2 came out in 1671.)

CERVANTES SAAVEDRA, MIGUEL DE. The second part of the History of the valorous and witty-knight-errant; Don Quixote, of The Mancha. R. Hodginson. (This title-page occurs on sig. Mm2 of the 1675 edition (Wing C1777). Fourth appearance of Shelton's translation.)

DELONEY, THOMAS. The gentle craft. Part I. (Wing D955 (no imprint given). Tenth edition.)

DELONEY, THOMAS. The pleasant history of John Winchcomb, in his yonger years called Jack of Newbery. Now the thirteenth time imprinted. E. Crouch, for T. Passinger. (Wing D963. Fourteenth edition.)

DELONEY, THOMAS. Thomas of Reading. For W. Thackeray. (Wing D966. Eighth edition.)

DESJARDINS, MARIE CATHERINE HORTENSE, Mme de Villedieu. The memoires of the life, and rare adventures of Henrietta Silvia Moliere. For

W. Crook. (Wing D1191. —Volume 1 only; v. 2 appeared in 1677.)

FORDE, EMANUEL. The most famous, delectable and pleasant history of Parismus. The second part. E. Crowch for F. Coles, T. Vere, and J. Wright. (Wing F1534. —Volume 2 only; volume 1 appeared the preceding year. —Thirteenth edition.)

FRENCH ROGUE. The French rogue. Being a pleasant history of his life and fortune. T. N. for S. Lowndes. (Wing F885. —Wrongly attributed to Charles de Fieux and Richard Head.)

GESTA ROMANORUM. A record of ancient historyes, entituled in Latine, Gesta Romanorum. E. Crowch, for A. Crook. (Wing R636. Seventeenth edition.)

GESTA ROMANORUM. A record of ancient histories, entituled in Latine, Gesta Romanorum. For F. Coles. (Esdaile. Eighteenth edition.)

GOLDEN EAGLE. The history of the Golden-Eagle. Written by Philaquila. For W. Thackeray. (Wing H2161. First edition.)

HEAD, RICHARD. The English rogue described, in the life of Meriton Latroon. For F. Kirkman. (Gibson's bibliography of Kirkman describes five issues of this edition, the eighth.)

KEPPLE, JOSEPH. The maiden-head lost by moon-light: or, The adventures of the meadow. For N. Brooke. (Wing K332A)

LAZARILLO DE TORMES. The pursuit of the history of Lazarillo de Tormes. R. Hodgkinson. (Esdaile; Yale University Library. —Possibly both parts appeared this year, but in all known copies this 2d part accompanies a 1st part dated 1677. —Ninth edition.)

OVID. Chaucer's ghoast . . . Containing twelve pleasant fables of Ovid [in verse] . . . With the history of Prince Corniger, and his champion Sir Crucifrag [in prose]. By a lover of antiquity [i.e. Charles Cotton?]. T. Ratcliff and N. Thompson for R. Mills. (Wing O647)

REYNARD THE FOX. A continuation, or, second part, of the Most pleasant and delightful history of Reynard the Fox. A. M. for E. Brewster. (Wing C5974. First edition of this part.)

SIDNEY, Sir PHILIP. The most excellent history of Argalus and Parthenia. A. P. for T. Vere. (Esdaile. First edition.)

1673

BELLIANIS. The famous and delectable history of Don Bellianis of Greece, or, The honour of chivalry, now newly written by Francis Kirkman. For F. Kirkman. 3 pts. (Wing F779 (pt.1). Fifth edition of part 1, third of part 2, second of part 3.)

DESJARDINS, MARIE CATHERINE HORTENSE, Mme de Villedieu. The loves of sundry philosophers and other great men. Translated out of French. T. N. for H. Herringham and J. Starkey. (Wing D1190)

FORDE, EMANUEL. The famous history of Montelyon. A. P. for W. Thackeray and T. Passinger. (Wing F1536. Seventh edition.)

FRITH, JOHN. The witty jests and mad pranks of John Frith commonly called the merry-conceited-mason. For T. Passenger. (Wing W3239A)

HEAD, RICHARD. The floating island: or, A new discovery. [London], Printed. (Wing H1253)

HEAD, RICHARD. News from the stars, by Meriton Latroon. (Cited by Esdaile, without imprint, from Lowndes.)

INGELO, NATHANIEL. Bentivolio and Urania. The third edition. T. R. for R. Marriott, sold by B. Tooke. (Wing I177. Third edition. —Some copies have variant imprint, either omitting Tooke's name (Wing I180), or adding that of T. Sawbridge.)

KIRKMAN, FRANCIS. The unlucky citizen . . . intermixed with severall choice novels. A. Johnson for K. Kirkman. (Wing K638)

LE PAYS, RENE. The drudge: or The jealous extravagant. For H. Herringman. (Wing L1115. —Epistle dedicatory signed J. B.)

PATRICK, SIMON. The parable of the pilgrim. The fourth edition. R. White for F. Tyton. (Wing P830. Fifth edition.)

QUEVEDO Y VILLEGAS, FRANCISCO DE. Visions. Made English by R[oger] L[Estrange]. The fifth edition corrected. For H. Herringman. (Wing Q199. Sixth edition.)

SACK-FULL OF NEWS. The sack-full of newes. A. Clark, sold by T. Passenger. (Wing S223. First known edition; entered SR 1557/58.)

SEVEN SAGES. The history of the seven wise masters of Rome. E. Crowh [sic] for J. Wright. (Harvard University Library. Eighth edition.)

VALENTINE AND ORSON. The famous history of Valentine and Orson. Written [i.e. abridged] by Laurence Price. For W. Whitwood. (Wing H3797 and P3361. First edition of this abridgment.)

ABU BAKR IBN AL-TUFAIL, ABU JAFAR. An account of the Oriental philosophy, shewing . . . the profound wisdom of Hai Ebn Yokdan. [London], Printed. (Wing A150. —Translated by George Keith from Pocock's Latin version of the original Arabic.)

BERNARD, RICHARD. The isle of of man. The fifteenth edition. Glasgow. (Wing B2029. Sixteenth edition.)

CAVENDISH, MARGARET, Duchess of Newcastle. Natures pictures drawn by fancies pencil to the life. Being several feigned stories . . . The second edition. (Cited by Esdaile, without imprint, from Lowndes. Another issue of the second edition?)

CERIZIERS, RENE DE. The innocent lady, or The illustious innocence. The second edition. For W. Lee. (Wing C1680. Second edition.)

DELONEY, THOMAS. The gentle craft. The honour of the gentle craft expressed in three stories. A. Clark. (Esdaile. Eleventh edition.)

FAIR ONE OF TUNIS. The fair one of Tunis: or, The generous mistress. Out of French. For H. Brome. (Wing F102. —By Charles Cotton?)

FAUST. The historie of the damnable life and deserved death of Doctor John Faustus. For W. Whitwood. (Wing H2152. Seventh edition.)

FAUST. The second report of Doctor John Faustus. For W. Whitwood. [1674?] (Cited by Esdaile from an advertisement in pt. 1 of the same year. Third edition; first two editions in 1594.)

GRISELDA. The true and admirable history of Patient Grisel. For W.

Thackeray. (Wing T2412. Fourth edition. —Esdaile cites as another edition the British Museum copy printed for W. Thackeray [date cut off].)

HEAD, RICHARD. The complaisant companion, or New jests . . . and pleasant novels. H. B. (Term Catalogues. First edition; subsequent editions appeared as *Nugae venales*.)

HEAD, RICHARD. The English rogue. Continued in the life of Meriton Latroon. The third part. A. Johnson for F. Kirkman. (Wing H1250. Second edition of this part.)

HEAD, RICHARD. The western wonder: or, O Brazeel, an inchanted island discovered. For N. C. (Wing H1277)

HIND, JAMES. No jest like a true jest: being a compendious record of the merry life, and mad exploits of Capt. James Hind. A. P. for T. Vere. (Wing N1178. Second edition.)

LA CALPRENEDE, GAUTIER DE COSTES, sieur de. Hymen's Praeludia or loves master-peice [sic]. W. R. and J. R., sold by P. Parker and T. Guy. (Wing L123. Fourth edition.)

PASQUIN. Pasquin risen from the dead. J. C. for N. C. (Wing P656)

PRICE, LAURENCE. Witty VVilliam of VVilt-shire. For C. Passinger. (Wing P3394)

SAINT REAL, CESAR VICHARD DE. Don Carlos. Written in French . . . and newly Englished by H. I. T. N. for H. Herringman, and J. Crump. (Wing S353. First edition.)

SCUDERY, MADELEINE DE. Ibrahim, or The illustrious bassa. The whole work . . . now Englished by Henry Cogan, Gent. J. R., sold by

P. Parker, and T. Guy. (Wing S2161. Second edition.)

SEVEN SAGES. The history of Prince Erastus . . . and those famous philosophers called the seven wise masters of Rome. Written originally in Italian, then translated into French, and now rendred English by F[rancis] K[irkman]. A. Johnson for F. Kirkman. (Wing H2136. First appearance of this version.)

SIDNEY, Sir PHILIP. The Countess of Pembroke's Arcadia. The thirteenth edition. For G. Calvert. (Wing S3770. Sixteenth edition.)

TOM THE SHOEMAKER. The pleasant history of Tom the shoomaker. For I. Hose. 2 pts. (Wing P2552)

1675

BARNES, JOSHUA. Gerania: a new discovery of a little sort of people anciently discoursed of, called pigmies. W. G. for O. Blagrave. (Wing B870)

BERALDUS. Beraldus, Prince of Savoy. Translated out of French by a person of quality. For W. Grantham, and J. Crump. (Wing B1946)

BOURSAULT, EDME. The Prince of Conde. Made English. For H. Herringman. (Wing B3860)

CERVANTES SAAVEDRA, MIGUEL DE. The history of the valorous and witty knight errant, Don Quixote, of The Mancha. Translated out of the Spanish. For R. Scot, T. Basset, J. Wright, R. Chiswell. (Wing C1777. Part 1 only; part 2 appeared in 1672. —The fourth appearance of Shelton's translation.)

DELONEY, THOMAS. The pleasant and princely history of the gentle craft. [1675?] For H. Rhodes. (Wing D960. Twelfth edition.)

DESJARDINS, MARIE CATHERINE HORTENSE, Mme de Villedieu. The amours of the Count de Dunois made English. For W. Cademan. (Wing D1187)

GEORGE, St. The life and death of the famous champion of England, St. George. For W. Thackeray. (Esdaile. Second edition.)

GREENE, ROBERT. The pleasant history of Dorastus and Fawnia. (Cited by Esdaile, without imprint, from the *Censura Literaria*. Fourteenth edition.)

HEAD, RICHARD. The miss display'd, with all her wheedling arts and circumventions. To be sold by the booksellers. (Wing H1264. First edition.)

HEAD, RICHARD. Nugae venales: or a Complaisant companion. Being new jests . . . The second edition. W. D. (Wing H1266. Second edition.)

HICKATHRIFT, T H O M A S. The pleasant history of Thomas Hic-ka-thrift. J. M. for W. Thackeray and T. Passinger. [ca.1675?] (Esdaile, who cites also an edition listed by Hazlitt with imprint: For W. Thackeray.)

JOHNSON, RICHARD. The famous history of the seven champions of Christendom. R. W. for T. Bassett. 2v. (Wing J798. Tenth edition.)

JOHNSON, RICHARD. The most illustrious history of the seven champions of Christendom. For W. Whitwood. (Wing J811. Second edition of this abridgment.)

MACHIAVELLI, N I C C O L O. The marriage of Belphegor. (In: The works of the famous Nicolas Machi-

avel. For J. Starkey. Wing M128. Third edition. —Appeared also appended to Quevedo's *Visions*; see below.)

MONTFORT, FRANÇOIS SALVAT, sieur de. The circle: or Conversations on love and gallantry; originally in French: now Englished. By Nath. Noel, Gent. Printed in the year. (Wing N1218)

PRICE, LAURENCE. The witch of the woodlands; or, The Coblers new translation. A. P. for W. Thackeray. [ca.1675] (Esdaile. Second edition.)

QUEVEDO Y VILLEGAS, FRANCIS-CO DE. The town adventurer. For G. Baile, sold by H. Eversden. (Wing Q194)

QUEVEDO Y VILLEGAS, FRANCI-CO DE. Visions, to which is added The marriage of Belphegor. (Huntnigton Library. Seventh edition.)

SEVEN SAGES. W i s d o m s cabinet open'd: or, The famous history of the seven wise masters of Rome. (Esdaile. An abridgment, without imprint; arbitrarily dated by being placed here.)

SHIRLEY, JOHN. The famous history of Aurelius, the valiant London prentice. By J. S. (Cited by Esdaile with question mark from a fragment in the Bodleian. First edition? —Arbitrarily dated by being placed here.)

VAIRASSE, DENIS. The history of the Sevarites or Sevirambi . . . Written by one Captain Siden. For H. Brome. (Wing V20. First edition. —Part 1 only.)

VALENTINE AND ORSON. Valentine and Orson, the two sons of the Emperour of Greece. A. Purslow, for T. Passinger. [1675?] (Esdaile; Clark Library. Eighth edition.)

AESOP. The fables of Aesop. Sold by T. Fabian. (Cited by Esdaile from the Term Catalogues. —Caxton's version; the 28th of 40 editions of the fables in English during the period down to 1700.)

BACON, Sir FRANCIS. New Atlantis. (In: Sylva sylvarum. The tenth edition. S. G. and B. Griffin, for T. Lee. Wing B332. Twelfth edition.)

BERNARD, RICHARD. The isle of man. The fifteenth edition. For J. Wright and T. Sawbridge. (Cited by Esdaile from the Term Catalogues. Probably to be identified with Wing B2030, 1677, as below.)

BLIND BEGGAR. The history of the blind beggar of Bednal green. For F. Coles, T. Vere, and J. Wright. [ca.1676?] (Esdaile. First edition? —Arbitrarily dated by being placed here.)

BLIND BEGGAR. The history of the blind beggar of Bednal green. For F. Coles, T. Vere, J. Wright, and J. Clarke. [ca.1676?] (Esdaile. Second edition? —Arbitrarily dated by being placed here.)

BOYLE, ROGER, Earl of Orrery. English adventures. By a person of honour. T. Newcomb, for H. Herringman. (Wing O476)

BOYLE, ROGER, Earl of Orrery. Parthenissa. That most fam'd romance. The six volumes compleat. T. N. for H. Herringman. (Wing O490. First complete edition. —Parts had appeared from 1651 to 1669).

BREMOND, GABRIEL DE. Hattige: or The amours of the King of Tamaran. For R. Bentley. (Wing B4350. First edition.)

DELONEY, THOMAS. The gentle craft. (Esdaile, without imprint. Thirteenth edition.)

FORTUNATUS. The right, pleasant, and variable tragical history of Fortunatus. First penned in the Dutch tongue . . . and now first of all published in English; by T. C. A. Purslow, for G. Saubridge. (Wing R1509. First appearance of this version. —T. C. is sometimes identified as Thomas Churchyard.)

GLANVILLE, JOSEPH. Essays on several important subjects in philosophy and religion. J. D. for J. Baker and H. Mortlock. (Wing G809. —The seventh essay is a continuation of the *New Atlantis*.)

GUILLET DE ST. GEORGE, GEORGES. An account of a late voyage to Athens . . . By Monsieur de la Guillatiere. Now Englished. J. M. for H. Herringman. (Wing G2218)

JOHNSON, RICHARD. The famous history of the seven champions of Christendom. (Esdaile, without imprint. Eleventh edition.)

LA CALPRENEDE, GAUTIER DE COSTES, sieur de. Cassandra: the fam'd romance. Elegantly rendred into English by Sir Charles Cotterell. For P. Parker. (Wing L110. Fifth edition.)

LEFEVRE, RAOUL. The destruction of Troy. The ninth edition. For T. Passenger. (Wing L931, L936, L940. Eleventh edition.)

MAZARIN, HORTENSE (MANCINI) DE LA PORTE, duchesse de. The memoires of the Dutchess Mazarine. Written in French by her own hand, and done into English By P. Porter, Esq; W. Cademan. (Wing S355.

First edition. —Sometimes ascribed to the Abbé Saint Réal, and to others.)

MAZARIN, HORTENSE (MANCINI) DE LA PORTE, duchess de. The memoires of the Dutchess Mazarine. The second impression. W. Cademan. (Library of Congress. Second edition.) (Wing M1538)

MONTFORT, FRANÇOIS SALVAT, sieur de. The circle: or Conversations on love and gallantry. . . . For the author, sold by J. Carre, R. Hunt, and G. Miller. (Wing N1219, M2496. —Reissue of 1675 edition with cancel-title.)

PORT DULL. A new discoverie of an old traveller lately arrived from Port-Dul. Printed in the year 1676. (Wing N624)

SAINT REAL, CESAR VICHARD DE. Don Carlos. Newly Englished by H. I. The second edition. J. G. for H. Herringman and J. Crump. (Wing S354. Second edition.)

SCARRON, PAUL. Scarron's Comical romance: or, A facetious history of a company of strowling stage-players. Now turn'd into English. J. C. for W. Crooke. (Wing S831. Second edition. —Many changes in text from 1665.)

SUMMERS, WILL. A pleasant history of the life and death of Will Summers. For T. Vere, and J. Wright. (Wing P2551. Second edition.)

TACHMAS. Tachmas, Prince of Persia: an historical novel. Render'd into English by P. Porter, Esq. For D. Newman. (Wing T100)

VOTURE, VINCENT. Zelinda: an excellent new romance. Translated from the French of Monsieur De Scudery [sic]. By T. D. Gent. By T.

R. and N. T. for J. Magnes and R. Bentley. (Wing V684)

1677

BACON, Sir FRANCIS. New Atlantis. (In: Sylva sylvarum. The tenth edition. S. G. and B. Griffin, for T. Lee. Wing B333. A second issue of the 1676 edition.)

BERNARD, RICHARD. The isle of man. The fifteenth edition. R. E. for J. Wright. (Wing B2030. Seventeenth edition.)

BERNARD, RICHARD. The isle of man. The fifteenth edition. For W. Bromwich. (Wing B2030A. Eighteenth edition.)

BREMOND, GABRIEL DE. The cheating gallant, or The false Count Brion. For J. Magnes and R. Bentley. (Wing B4345)

BREMOND, GABRIEL DE. The happy slave. A novel. Translated from the French. By a person of quality. For J. Magnes and R. Bentley. 2v. (Wing B4348 (pt.1), B4349A (pt.2). First edition.)

CAMUS, JEAN PIERRE. A true tragical history of two illustrious Italian families. Done into English, by a person of quality. For W. Jacob. (Wing C419. First edition.)

CAPELLO AND BIANCA. Capello and Bianca. A novel. Written in French: and now Englished by L. N., Gent. For E. Wyer. (Cited by Esdaile from the Term Catalogues.)

DESJARDINS, MARIE CATHERINE HORTENSE, Mme de Villedieu. The disorders of love. Made English from the French. For J. Magnes and R. Bentley. (Wing D1188)

DESJARDINS, MARIE CATHERINE HORTENSE, Mme de Villedieu. The memoires of . . . Henrietta Silvia Moliere. The second volume. J. C. for W. Crooke. (Wing D1192. —Volume 1 appeared in 1672.)

FAUST. The history of the damnable life and deserved death of Doctor John Faustus. For T. Sawbridge. (Cited by Esdaile from the Term Catalogues. —Eighth edition.)

FORDE, EMANUEL. The famous history of Montelyon. Sold by W. Trackeray and T. Passenger. (Wing F1527. Eighth edition.)

FORDE, EMANUEL. The most famous, delectable, and pleasant history of Parismus. For F. Coles, T. Vere, J. Wright, and J. Clarke. 2v. (Esdaile; McLeish 98:104. Fourteenth edition.)

FORDE, EMANUEL. The most renowned and pleasant history of Parismus. By A. P. and T. H. for F. Coles, T. Vere, J. Wright, and J. Clarke. (Wing F1534. An abridgment.)

GOLDEN EAGLE. The history of the Golden Eagle. . . Written by Philaquila. For W. Thackeray. (Wing H2162. Second edition.)

GREENE, ROBERT. The pleasant history of Dorastus and Fawnia. For J. Wright, sold by J. Clarke. (Wing G1836. Fifteenth edition.)

HEAD, RICHARD. The life and death of Mother Shipton. For B. Harris. (Wing H1257. Second edition.)

HERBERAY, NICOLAS DE. The most excellent history of . . . Don Flores of Greece. For W. Thackeray. (Cited by Esdaile from an advertisement of Thackeray's in this year.

—See also under 1664.)

L., L. Evagoras, a romance. By L. L., Gent. For R. Clavel and T. More. (Wing L40)

LA CALPRENEDE, GAUTIER DE COSTES, sieur de. Pharamond: or, The history of France. Translated by J. Phillips, Gent. For T. Bassett, T. Dring, and W. Cademan. (Wing L126. —First appearance of this translation.)

LA ROCHE GUILHEM, Mlle. de. Asteria and Tamberlain; or The distressed lovers. Rendred into English by E. C. Esq. For R. Sollers. (Wing L447. First edition.)

LAZARILLO DE TORMES. Lazarillo: or, The excellent history of Lazarillo de Tormes, the witty Spaniard. E. Hodginson. 2v. (Wing L763. —Part 2 of this edition (the ninth) is dated 1672 in all known copies, though there may have been an edition of both parts in 1677.)

MANDEVILLE, Sir JOHN. The voyages and travels of Sir John Mandevile knight. For R. Scott, T. Basset, J. Wright, and R. Chiswell. (Wing M415. Sixteenth edition.)

MONTELION, pseud. Don Juan Lamberto, or A comical history of the late times. W. Thackeray. (Cited by Esdaile from an advertisement. Fifth edition.)

POOR ROBIN. Poor Robin's Visions: wherein is described, the present humours of the times. A. Boldero. (Wing H1598. —Usually ascribed to William Winstanley.)

PRICE, LAURENCE. The witch of the woodlands. For W. T[hackeray], sold by C. Passinger. [1677?] (Wing P3393. Third edition?)

SCUDERY, MADELEINE DE. Almahide; or, The captive queen. Done
into English by J. Phillips Gent. J.
M. for T. Dring. (Wing S2142)

SCUDERY, MADELAINE DE. Clelia.
An excellent new romance. The
fourth [-fifth] volume[s]. Rendered
into English by G[eorge] H[avers].
For D. Newman, and T. Cockerell.
(Wing S2156. Second edition. —Volume 5 has imprint: For H. Herringman. —Volumes 1-3 appeared in 1678.)

SEVEN SAGES. The history of the
seven wise masters of Rome. For J.
Wright. (Wing H2182. Ninth edition.)

VALENTINE AND ORSON. Valentine and Orson, the two sons of the
Emperour of Greece. (Cited by Esdaile with question mark from Hazlitt (without imprint). Ninth edition.)

1678

ALCOFORADO, M A R I A N N A D'.
Five love-letters from a nun to a cavalier. Done out of French into English. For H. Brome. (Wing A889.
First edition. —Although tradition-
ally ascribed to Alcoforado, the work
is almost certainly by Gabriel-Joseph
de Lavergne Guilleragues.)

A L T O P H E L AND ASTREA. A
pleasant novel, discovering the humours and intrigues of a town gallant, in the delectable amours of
Altophel and Astrea. For W. Leach.
(Cited by Esdaile from the Term
Catalogues.)

BELLIANIS. The honour of chivalry.
Or, The famous and delectable history of Don Bellianis of Greece. For
T. Passinger. (Esdaile; Clark Library. Sixth edition. —Part 1 only.)

BREMOND, GABRIEL DE. The
happy slave, a pleasant novel. In
three parts compleat. Rendred into
English by a person of quality. T.
R. and N. T. for J. Magnes and R.
Bentley. (Wing B4348A, B4349B
(pt.3). Second edition; first appearance of the 3d part.)

BREMOND, GABRIEL DE. The
triumph of love over fortune. Translated into English by a person of
quality. For J. Magnes and R. Bentley. (Wing B4357)

BREMOND, GABRIEL DE. The viceroy of Catalonia, or The double
cuckold. Made English by James
Morgan, Gent. J. B. for J. Magnes
and R. Bentley. (Wing B4358. First
edition.)

BUNYAN, J O H N. The pilgrim's
progress. For N. Ponder. (Wing
B5557. First edition.)

BUNYAN, J O H N. The pilgrim's
progress. The second edition. For N.
Ponder. (Wing B5558. Second edition.)

CAMUS, JEAN P I E R R E. Forced
marriage. . . . Truly represented in
the downfall of two illustrious Italian families. The second impression.
For W. Jacob. (Wing C414. —First
issued in 1677 as *A true tragical history of two illustrious Italian families.*)

DELONEY, THOMAS. The first part
of the pleasant and princely history
of the gentle craft. T. M. for W.
Thackery. (Wing D944. Fourteenth
edition.)

HEYWOOD, THOMAS. The famous
and remarkable history of Sir Richard Whittington. Written by T. H.
A. P. and T. H. for T. Vere and J.
Wright. (Wing H1781. Second edition.)

LA FAYETTE, MARIE MADELEINE, comtesse de. Zayde, a Spanish history. Originally written in French, by Monsieur Segray. Done into English by P. Porter, Esq; T. Milbourn for W. Cademan. 2v. (Wing L172, L173A. First edition. —Some copies have variant imprint: For W. Cademan. [Wing L172A].)

LA ROCHE GUILHEM, Mlle de. Almanzor and Almanzaida. A novel. Written by Sir Philip Sidney, And found since his Death amongst his Papers. For J. Magnes and R. Bentley, (Wing L446)

MRS. MONEY. The death and burial of Mistress Money. A. Clark, sold by T. Vere and J. Clark. (Wing D501. Second edition.)

OBLIGING MISTRESS. The obliging mistress: or, The fashionable gallant. By a person of quality. For J. Magnes, and R. Bentley. (Wing O89)

PATRICK, SIMON. The parable of the pilgrim. The fifth edition. R. White for F. Tyton. (Wing P831. Sixth edition.)

PRECHAC, JEAN DE. The English princess, or The dutchess queen. A novel. In two parts. For W. Cademan and S. Neale. (Wing E3115. First edition.)

PRECHAC, JEAN DE. The heroine musqueteer, or The female warrier. [Parts 1-2.] For J. Magnes and R. Bentley, and R. Tonson. (Wing P3206, P3208. First edition. —Parts 3-4 appeared following year.)

QUEVEDO Y VILLEGAS, FRANCICO DE. Visions. Made English by R[oger] L[Estrange]. The sixth edition corrected. For H. Herringman. (Wing Q200. Eighth edition.)

ROBIN HOOD. The noble birth and gallant atchievements of . . . Robin Hood. (Wing N1202 (without imprint). Second edition.)

SCUDERY, MADELEINE DE. Clelia, an excellent new romance: the whole work in five parts. H. Herringman, D. Newman, T. Cockerel [etc.] (Wing S2156. Second edition. —Translated by John Davies. —Parts 4-5 (translated by George Havers) dated 1677.)

SUBLIGNY, ADRIEN THOMAS PERDOU DE. The mock-Clelia: being a comical history of French gallantries, and novels, in imitation of Dom Quixote. Translated out of French. For L. Curtis. (Wing S6107. —Some copies have variant imprint: For L. C., sold by S. Neale and C. Blount.)

TUDOR, OWEN. Tudor, a prince of Wales. An historical novel. In two parts. H. H., for J. Edwin. (Wing T3220)

VILLAINS. The lives of sundry notorious villains . . . Together with a novel, as it really happened at Roan in France. For the author, sold by S. Crouch. (Wing B1739. Probably same as the edition cited by Esdaile from the Term Catalogues, 1678. —By Aphra Behn?)

VILLIERS, CLAUDE DESCHAMPS, sieur de. The gentleman apothecary. Turn'd out of French. Sold by H. Brome. (Cited by Esdaile from the Term Catalogues. Second edition.)

VOITURE, VINCENT. Alcidalis. (In: A collection of select discourses out of the most eminent wits of France and Italy. S. R. for H. Brome. (Wing C5191.)

AMOROUS CONVERT. The amorous convert. Being a true relation of what happened in Holland. R. E. for R. Tonson. (Wing A3019)

BAYLY, THOMAS. The wall-flower. As it grew out of the stone chamber . . . By I. G., sold by P. Parker. (Wing B1516. Second edition; first edition appeared as *Herba parietis*.)

BUNYAN, JOHN. The pilgrim's progress. The third edition. For N. Ponder. (Wing B5559. Third edition.)

CARLETON, ROWLAND. D i a n a, Dutchess of Mantua: or The persecuted lover. T. H., sold by H. Brome. (Wing C587. First edition.)

COLONNA, MARIA (MANCINI). The apology: or, The genuine memoires of Madam Maria Manchini, Constabless of Colonna. Written in Spanish by her own hand, and afterwards made into English by a person of quality. For J. Magnes and R. Bentley. (Wing B4344. —Possibly written by Gabriel de Bremond.)

DEMOCRATES. Fatall prudence, or, Democrates, the unfortunate heroe. A novell. Translated out of French. J. Bennet for R. Bentley and M. Magnes. (Wing F544)

DESJARDINS, MARIE CATHERINE HORTENSE, Mme de Villedieu. The unfotunate [sic] heroes: or, The adventures of ten famous men. Englished by a gentleman for his diversion. T. N. for H. Herringman. (Wing D1193)

ENGLISH MONSIEUR. The English monsieur. A comical novel. For W. Cademan. (Esdaile)

FORTUNATUS. The right, pleasant, and variable tragical history of Fortunatus. By T. C. For G. Sawbridge. (Cited by Esdaile, with question mark, from the Term Catalogues. Second appearance of this version.)

FRIAR BACON. The famous history of Friar Bacon. M. Clark, sold by T. Passenger. (Wing F373. Seventh edition.)

HEAD, RICHARD. The life and death of the English rogue. For C. Passinger. (Wing H1262. An abridgment of part 1 of *The English rogue.*)

JOHNSON, RICHARD. The renowned history of the seven champions of Christendom. A. P. and T. H. for T. Vere. (Esdaile. —An abridgment.)

LA FAYETTE, MARIE MADELEINE, comtesse de. The Princess of Cleves. Englished by a person of quality. For R. Bentley and M. Magnes. (Wing L169. First edition.)

PENITENT HERMIT. The penitent hermit, or The fruits of jealousie; being a true and witty relation of a pleasant adventure. In two parts. For W. Cademan. (Wing P1233)

PRECHAC, JEAN DE. The third and fourth parts of The heroine musqueter. For J. Magnes and R. Bentley, and R. Tonson. (Wing P3208B. First edition. —Parts 1-2 appeared the preceding year.)

REYNOLDS, JOHN. The triumphs of Gods revenge. The sixth edition. To which is added, Gods revenge against the abominable sin of adultery. J. Bennet, for T. Lee. (Wing R1313. Tenth edition. —Epistle dedicatory signed S. Pordage.)

VAIRASSE, DENIS. The history of the Sevarites, or Sevarambi. The second part. By J. M. for H. Brome. (Wing V20A. First edition. —Part 1 appeared in 1675.)

1680

ALCOFORADO, M A R I A N N A D'. Five love-letters from a nun to a cavalier. Done out of French into English. For H. Brome. (Wing A890. Second edition.)

AULNOY, MARIE CATHERINE JU-MELLE DE BERNEVILLE, comtesse d'. The novels of Elizabeth Queen of England; containing the history of Queen Ann of Bullen. Faithfully rendred into English by S[pencer] H[ickman]. For M. Pardoe. (Wing A4221. —Part 1; the second part appeared in 1681.)

BREMOND, GABRIEL DE. Hattige: or The amours of the King of Tamaran. Amsterdam [i.e. London]: For Simon the African [i.e. R. Bentley?]. (Wing B4351. Second edition.)

BREMOND, GABRIEL DE. The pilgrim. Translated into English by P. Bellon, Gent. For R. Bentley and M. Magnes. (Wing B4353. First edition. —The second volume, a continuation by Bellon, appeared in 1681.)

BREMOND, G A B R I E L DE. The princess of Montferrat. For R. Bently and M. Magnes. (Wing B4355. —Part 1 only; part 2 appeared in 1681. —Dedication signed E. S.)

BUNYAN, JOHN. The life and death of Mr. Badman. J. A. for N. Ponder. (Wing B5550. First edition.)

BUNYAN, J O H N. The pilgrim's progress. The fourth edition. For N. Ponder. (Wing B5560. Fourth edi-

tion. —Another issue of the same edition appeared the same year. Wing B5561.)

BUNYAN, J O H N. The pilgrim's progress. The fifth edition. For N. Ponder. (Wing B5562. Fifth edition.)

BUNYAN, J O H N. The pilgrim's progress. The fifth edition. Edinburgh: I. Cairns. (Wing B5563. Sixth edition.)

DANGERFIELD, T H O M A S. Don Tomazo, or The juvenile rambles of Thomas Dangerfield. For W. Rumbald. (Wing D185)

EDWARD, the Black Prince. The Conquest of France, with the life, and glorious actions of Edward the Black Prince. A. M. for C. Bates. [1680?] (Wing C5895. —Date taken from Wing; very dubious.)

ELIZABETH, Queen. The secret history of the most renowned Q. Elizabeth, and the E. of Essex. Cologne [i.e. London]: For Will with the wisp [i.e. R. Bentley]. 2v. (Wing S2342. First edition. —Wing lists another edition (S2342A), with imprint: Cologne, For the Man in the moon, and Will of the wisp, which he dates [168-?]. Second edition.)

FAUST. The second report of Doctor John Faustus. For R. Smith. (Wing S2331. Fourth edition.)

FORDE, EMANUEL. The famous history of Montelyon. W. Thackeray and T. Passinger. (Wing F1528. Ninth edition.)

HEAD, R I C H A R D. The English rogue. [Parts 1-4]. For F. Kirkman, sold by W. Rands. (Wing H1251. Second edition of all four parts together.)

HENRIETTA, Princess. The amours of Madame, and the Count de Guiche. Translated into English, by a person of quality. For B. C: Obedience [i.e. R. Bentley and W. Cademan]. (Wing A3022)

HENRY VIII. The cobler turned courtier. Being a pleasant humour between King Henry the Eighth and a cobler. For F. Haley. (Wing C4782. First edition.)

HEYWOOD, THOMAS. The famous and remarkable history of Sir Richard Whittington. For W. Thackeray and T. Passinger. [ca.1680] (Wing H1782. Third edition.)

HIND, JAMES. No jest like a true jest. . . . T. H. for T. Vere. (Wing N1179. Third edition.)

JOHNSON, RICHARD. The famous history of the seven champions of Christendom. For R. Scot, T. Basset, J. Wright, and R. Chiswell. 2v. (Wing J802A. Twelfth edition.)

LA ROCHE GUILHEM, Mlle de. Royal lovers: or, The unhappy prince. For R. Sollers. (Wing L449. Second edition; first edition appeared in 1677 as *Asteria and Tamberlain*.)

LEFEVRE, RAOUL. The destruction of Troy. The tenth edition. For T. Passinger. (Wing L932, L937, L941. Twelfth edition.)

MACHIAVELLI, N I C C O L O. The marriage of Belphegor. (In: The works of the famous Nicholas Machiavel. For J. Starkey, C. Harper, and J. Amery. Wing M129. Fifth edition.)

MONTFAUCON DE VILLARS. The Count of Gabalis: or, The extravagant mysteries of the cabalists. Done into English, by P[hilip] A[yres] Gent. For B. M. [i.e. Bentley and Magnes]. (Wing M2494)

MONTFAUCON DE VILLARS. The Count of Gabalis: or, Conferences about secret sciences. Rendered out of French into English . . . by A[rchibald] L[ovell] A. M. For R. Harford. (Wing M2495)

NICOSTRATUS. Nicostratus. (Cited by Esdaile from an advertisement by Bentley and Magnes.)

PALAIS ROYAL. The history of the Palais Royal, or The amours of Mademoiselle de la Valiere. For R. Bentley and W. Cademan. (Term Catalogues, I, 393. First edition.)

PRECHAC, JEAN DE. The illustrious Parisian maid, or The secret amours of a German prince. For J. Amery. (Esdaile)

ROSAMOND. The life and death of Rosamond. For W. Thackeray and T. Passinger. [ca.1680] (Esdaile. Second edition.)

VALENTINE AND ORSON. The history of Valentine and Orson, the two sons of the Emperour of Greece. Sold by T. Passenger. (Cited by Esdaile, with question mark, from the Term Catalogues. Tenth edition.)

VICTORIOUS LOVERS. [The victorious lovers; or, Love victorious over fortune. R. Bentley?] [168-?] (Esdaile)

1681

ALCOFORADO, M A R I A N N A D'. Seven Portuguese letters: being a second part to the Five love-letters from a nun to a cavalier. For J. Brome. (Wing A893. First edition of this part.)

AULNOY, MARIE CATHERINE JUMELLE DE BERNEVILLE, comtesse d'. The novels of Elizabeth, Queen of England. Containing the history of Bassa Solyman, and the Princess Eronima. The last part. Englished by Spencer Hickman. E. T. and R. H. for M. Pardow. (Wing A4222. —First part appeared in 1680.)

BLESSEBOIS, PIERRE CORNEILLE. Aloisia, or, The amours of Octavia Englished, to which is adjoyned The history of Madam du Tillait. For J. Tonson. (Wing A2897A)

BREMOND, GABRIEL DE. Gallant memoirs: or The adventures of a person of quality. Translated into English, by P. Bellon. For R. Bentley and M. Magnes. (Wing B4347)

BREMOND, GABRIEL DE. The pilgrim. The second part. Written by P. Belon, Gent. Translator of the first part. For R. Bentley and M. Magnes. (Wing B1855. First appearance of this part, which is entirely the work of Bellon; part 1 appeared in 1680.)

BREMOND, GABRIEL DE. The princess of Montferrat. The second part. For R. Bentley and M. Magnes. (Wing B4356. —The general title-page for both parts is also dated 1681; title-page to part 1 is dated 1680.)

BUNYAN, JOHN. The pilgrim's progress. The fifth edition. For N. Ponder. (Esdaile. Seventh edition.)

BUNYAN, JOHN. The pilgrim's progress. Boston: S. Green. (Wing B5566. Eighth edition [first American edition].)

BUNYAN, JOHN. The pilgrim's progress. The sixth edition. For N. Ponder. (Wing B5564. Ninth edition.)

BUNYAN, JOHN. The pilgrim's progress. The seventh edition. For N. Ponder. (Wing B5565. Tenth edition.)

CARLETON, ROWLAND. The Italian princess, or Loves persecutions. A new romance. For H. Bonwicke. (Wing C588. —Actually the second edition of *Diana, Dutchess of Mantua*.)

CERVANTES SAAVEDRA, MIGUEL DE. The jealous gentleman of Estremadure. For C. Blount and R. Butt. (Esdaile)

COBBLER OF CANTERBURY. A witty, pleasant, and true discourse of the merry cobler of Canterbury; together with the pretty conceits of Frier Bacon. Edinburgh: (Cited by Esdaile from Hazlitt.)

CROUCH, NATHANIEL. Wonderful prodigies of judgment and mercy, discovered in above three hundred memorable histories. By R. B. (Cited by Esdaile, without imprint, from the *DNB*. First edition.)

ELIZABETH, Queen. The secret history of the most renowned Q. Elizabeth and the E. of Essex. The second edition. For R. Bentley and M. Magnes. 2v. (Wing S2343. Third edition?)

FORDE, EMANUEL. The most famous, delectable, and pleasant history of Parismus. The eleventh impression. T. H. for F. Coles, T. Vere, J. Wright, J. Clarke, W. Thackeray and T. Passenger. 2v. (Wing F1536. Fifteenth edition. —Volume 2 has imprint: M. White for T. Vere [etc.])

GESTA ROMANORUM. A record of ancient histories, intituled in Latine: Gesta Romanorum. T. H. for R. Scott, T. Bassett, R. Chiswell, and

J. Wright. (Wing R637. Nineteenth edition.)

GRACIAN Y MORALES, BALTASAR. The critick. Translated into English, by Paul Rycaut, Esq; T. N. for H. Brome. (Wing G1470)

GRENADINE, SEBASTIAN. Homais Queen of Tunis, a novel. Amsterdam [i.e. London]: For Simon the Afrikan [i.e. R. Bentley?]. (Wing G1935)

GRIMALKIN. Grimalkin, or, The rebel-cat. A novel. For the author. (Wing G2026)

GUY OF WARWICK. The renowned history, of The life and death of Guy Earl of Warwick. H. Brugis for P. Brooksby. (Wing S3515. First appearance of this version, with preface signed John Shurley.)

LA CHAPPELLE, JEAN DE. The unequal match; or, The life of Mary of Anjou Queen of Majorca. For C. Blount and R. Butt. (Wing L133. Volume 1 only; v. 2 appeared in 1683. —Dedication signed F. S., i.e. Ferrand Spence.)

LISANDER. Lisander or The souldier of fortune, a novel. H. H. for H. Faithorne and J. Kersey. (Wing L2366A)

OUDIN, CESAR FRANÇOIS. The extravagant poet. Translated out of French, by G. R. Gent. For B. M. [i.e. Bentley and Magnes]. (Wing O571)

PLOT IN A DREAM. The plot in a dream: or, The discoverer in masquerade. In a succinct discourse and narrative of the late and present designs of the Papists . . . T. Snowden for J. Hancock and E. Prosser. (Wing P2598)

PRECHAC, JEAN DE. The lovely Polander. For J. Kidgel. [1681] (Wing P3207A)

REYNARD THE FOX. The most delectable history of Reynard the Fox. A. M. and R. R. for E. Brewster. (Wing S3512. Fifteenth edition.)

REYNARD THE FOX. The most pleasant and delightful history of Reynard the Fox. The second part. A. M. and R. R. for E. Brewster. (Wing M2912. Second edition of this part.)

ROUSSEAU DE LA VALETTE, MICHEL. Casimir, King of Poland. For C. Smith. (Wing R2051)

SCUDERY, MADELEINE DE. Amaryllis to Tityrus. A witty and pleasant novel. Englished by a person of honour. For W. Cademan. (Wing S2143)

1682

ANTONIUS AND AURELIA. The most excellent history of Antonius and Aurelia: or, The two incomparable lovers. T. Haley, sold by J. Wright, J. Clarke, W. Thackeray, and T. Passenger. (Wing M2882)

BERNARD, CATHERINE. The female prince; or, Frederick of Sicily. In three parts. For H. Rodes. (Wing B1984. —Dedication signed F. S., i.e. Ferrand Spence.)

BUNYAN, JOHN. The holy war. For D. Newman and B. Alsop. (Wing B5538. First edition.)

BUNYAN, JOHN. The pilgrim's progress. The fifth [sic] edition. For N. Ponder. (Wing B5567. Eleventh edition.)

BUNYAN, JOHN. The pilgrim's progress. The eighth edition. For N.

Ponder. (Wing B5568. Twelfth edition.)

CROUCH, NATHANIEL. Wonderful prodigies of judgment and mercy, discovered in above three hundred memorable histories. By R. B. For N. Crouch. (Wing C7361. Second edition.)

FAUST. The history of the damnable life and deserved death of Doctor John Faustus. For T. Sawbridge. (Wing H2153. Ninth edition.)

FORTUNATUS. The history of the birth, travels, strange adventures, and death of Fortunatus. T. Haly. (Wing H2145. Second appearance of the [1650?] edition?)

FORTUNATUS. The right, pleasant, and variable trachical history of Fortunatus. First penned in the Dutch tongue . . . and now first of all published in English by T. C. T. B. for H. Sawbridge. (Wing R1510. Third edition of this version.)

FRIAR BACON. The history of Fryer Bacon. For T. Passenger. (Esdaile. Eighth edition.)

GESTA ROMANORUM. A record of ancient histories, entituled in Latine: Gesta Romanorum. (Cited by Esdaile without imprint. Twentieth edition.)

GRISELDA. The true and admirable history of Patient Grisel. For J. Wright, J. Clarke, W. Thackeray, and T. Passenger. (Wing T2413. Sixth edition.)

INGELO, NATHANIEL. Bentivolo and Urania. The fourth edition. A. M. and R. R. for D. Newman. (Wing I178. Fourth edition. —Some copies have variant imprint: E. T. and R. H. for D. Newman. (Wing I181))

INTRIGUES OF LOVE. The intrigues of love. A novel. Written originally in French, and newly translated into English by P. Lorrain. Sold by F. Gardiner. (Esdaile)

JOHNSON, RICHARD. The most pleasant history of Tom a Lincoln. The twelveth impression. H. Brugis for W. Thackeray. (Wing J808. Eleventh edition. —Also another edition, same year, with imprint: H. B. for W. Thackeray. (Wing J809) Twelfth edition.)

LOREDANO, GIOVANNI FRANCESCO. The novells. Translated for diversion into English. For T. Fox and H. Lord. (Wing L3068)

LOVE'S EMPIRE. Loves empire; or, The amours of the French court. For D. Newman. (Wing L3264A. —Reissued with other material in 1684 as *The history of the amours of the French court.*)

MEROVEUS. Mcroveus a prince of the blood-royal of France. A novel. For R. Bentley and M. Magnes. (Wing M1834)

OLDYS, ALEXANDER. The fair extravagant, or The humorous bride- An English novel. For C. Blount. (Folger Library. —Probably the edition Esdaile cites from the Term Catalogues for 1681.)

PASTIME ROYAL. The pastime royal; or, The gallantries of the French court. In two parts. By a person of quality. J. Harefinch for H. Rodes. (Wing P664)

PRECHAC, JEAN DE. The Princess of Fess: or, The amours of the court of Morocco. A novel. In two parts. For R. Bently, and M. Magnes. (Wing B1857 and P3207B. —Dedication signed P. Bellon.)

61

QUEVEDO Y VILLEGAS, FRANCIS-CO DE. Visions. The second part. Containing many strange and wonderful remarques. T. Haly. (Wing Q200A. First appearance of this part.)

QUEVEDO Y VILLEGAS, FRANCIS-CO DE. Visions. The second part. . . . The second edition with additions, corrected and amended by J. S. Gent. T. Haly. (Second edition)

REYNOLDS, JOHN. The triumphs of Gods revenge. To which is added, God's revenge against the abominable sin of adultery. For C. Passinger. (Esdaile. Eleventh edition.)

S., T. The perplex'd prince. For R. Allen. [1682?] (Wing S174. —Dedication signed T. S. —Esdaile also lists another undated edition, corrected.)

S., T. The second part of the Pilgrim's progress. T. H. (Wing S178. First edition. —Not by Bunyan; dedication signed T. S., i.e. Thomas Sherman?)

SEVEN SAGES. The history of the seven wise masters of Rome. For J. Wright. (Wing H2183. Tenth edition.)

VALENTINE AND ORSON. Valentine and Orson, the two sons of the Emperour of Greece. T. H. for T. Passinger. (Wing V29. Eleventh edition.)

1683

ADAMITE. The Adamite, or The loves of Father Rock. A famous novel, translated out of French. For D. Newman. (University of Illinois Library. —A second part is entitled *Conversations at the grate.* —Advertised again in 1698 as *The Adamite; or, The insensible Jesuit.*)

ARGENCES, D'. The Countess of Salisbury; or, The most noble order of the Garter. Done out of French by Mr. Ferrand Spence. For R. Bentley and S. Magnes. (Wing A3630. First edition.)

BACON, Sir FRANCIS. New Atlantis. (In: Sylva sylvarum. For B. Griffin. Wing B334. Second reissue of the 1676 edition.)

BARRIN, JEAN. Venus in the cloyster, or The nun in her smock. By the Abbot Du Prat [pseud.] Done out of French. For H. Rodes. —Term Catalogues, II, 19. —Also attributed to Chavigny de la Bretonnière.)

BEHN, APHRA. Love letters between a nobleman and his sister. For J. Hindmarsh. (Esdaile. First edition.)

BELLIANIS. The honour of chivalry. Or, The famous and delectable history of Don Bellianis of Greece. For T. Passinger. 3 pts. (Wing F780 (pt.1), S3507 (pts. 2-3). Seventh edition. —Parts 2-3 have separate title page and were written by J[ohn] S[hirley].)

BERNARD, RICHARD. The isle of man. The sixteenth edition. T. M. (Wing B2031. Nineteenth edition.)

BREMOND, GABRIEL DE. Hattige: or, The amours of the King of Tamaran. Amsterdam [London]: For Simon the African [i.e. R. Bentley?]. (Wing B4352. Third edition.)

BUNYAN, JOHN. The pilgrim's progress. The ninth edition. For N. Ponder. (Wing B5569. Thirteenth edition.)

CAWWOOD THE ROOK. The pleasant history of Cawwood the Rook. For J. Wright, J. Clarke, W. Thackeray and T. Passinger. (Wing P2549. Third edition. —Esdaile also lists, without imprint, another edition, imperfect. Fourth edition.)

CESPEDES Y MENESES, GONZALO DE. The famous history of Auristella. Together with the pleasant story of Paul of Segovia, by Don Francisco de Quevedo. For J. Hindmarsh. (Wing C1782)

CHAMBERLAYNE, WILLIAM. Eromena: or, The noble stranger, a novel. For J. Norris. (Wing C1864. —A prose version of his *Pharonnida*.)

CHAMILLY, NOEL BOUTON, marquis de. Five love-letters written by a cavalier, in answer to the five love-letters written to him by a nun. For R. Bentley and M. Magnes. (Wing F1110. First edition. —Caption title: The answers of the Chevalier Del.)

COLERAINE, HUGH HARE, 1st baron. The situation of Paradise found out: being an history of a late pilgrimage unto the Holy Land. J. C. and F. C. for S. Lowndes, and H. Faithorne, and J. Kersey. (Wing C5064)

CRAFTY LADY. The crafty lady: or The rival of himself. Translated out of French into English by F. C. Ph. Gent. For E. Vize. (Wing C6774)

CROUCH, NATHANIEL. The extraordinary adventures and discoveries of several famous men. By R. B. J. Richardson, for N. Crouch. (Wing C7323. First edition.)

CROUCH, NATHANIEL. The surprizing miracles of nature and art. By R. B. For N. Crouch. (Wing C7349. First edition.)

CROUCH, NATHANIEL. Unparallel'd varieties. For N. Crouch. (Wing C7352. First edition.)

DUNTON, JOHN. The informer's doom: or, An amazing and seasonable letter from Utopia, directed to the man in the moon. For J. Dunton. (Wing D2629. —Epistle dedicatory signed Philagathus.)

DUTCH ROGUE. The Dutch rogue or, Gusman of Amsterdam . . . being the life, rise, and fall of D. de Lebechea a decay'd merchant. Out of Nether-Dutch. A. M. for G. Hill. (Wing D2905)

FORDE, EMANUEL. The most pleasant history of Ornatus and Artesia. The eighth impression. M. White, for J. Wright, J. Clark, W. Thackeray, and T. Passenger. (Wing F1523. Eighth edition.)

FORDE, EMANUEL. The most renowned and pleasant history of Parismus. H. B. for J. Wright, J. Clark, W. Thackery, and T. Passenger. (Library of Congress. —An abridgment.)

FORTUNATE LOVERS. The fortunate, the deceived, and the unfortunate lovers. Three excellent new novels. For W. Cademan. (Esdaile. Cf. 1632. —Reissued in 1685 as *Three excellent new novels?*)

FRIAR BACON. The famous history of Fryer Bacon. For M. W. (Wing F374. Ninth edition.)

FUGITIVE STATESMAN. The fugitive statesman, in requital for the Perplex'd prince. A. Grover. (Wing F2259)

GERMONT, DE. The Neapolitan, or The defender of his mistress. Done out of French by Mr. Ferrand Spence. For R. Bentley. (Wing N361)

HEAD, RICHARD. The miss display'd, with all her wheedling arts and circumventions. (Wing H1265. Second edition.)

KEACH, BENJAMIN. The travels of True Godliness. For J. Dunton. (Wing K97. First edition.)

LA CHAPPELLE, JEAN DE. The unequal match: or, The life of Mary of Anjou Queen of Majorca. The second and last [i.e. third] part. For R. Bentley. (Wing L134. —Volume 1 appeared in 1681.)

LONDON BULLY. The London bully, or The prodigal son. H. Clark, for T. Malthus. 2v. (Wing L2890)

OLDYS, ALEXANDER. The London jilt: or, The politick whore. For H. Rodes. (Wing O266. First edition.)

RELIGIOUS CAVALIER. The religious cavalier. Done out of French. By Gideon Pierreville, Gent. J. H. for John Cripps. (Newberry Library)

S., T. The second part of the Pilgrims progress. For T. Malthus. (Wing S379. Second edition. —Not by Bunyan.)

SCARRON, PAUL. Scarron's Novels. For T. Basset, sold by W. Freeman. (Hazlitt. Third edition.)

SEBASTIAN. Don Sebastian King of Portugal. An historical novel. Done out of French by Mr. Ferrand Spence. For R. Bentley and S. Magnes. (Wing D1847)

SIDNEY, Sir PHILIP. The pleasant and delightful history of Argalus and Parthenia. T. H. for T. Passenger. (Wing Q112. Second edition.)

SUNDAY'S ADVENTURE. A Sundays adventure, or, Walk to Hackney. Being a description of an amorous intrigue acted there. For J. Kidgel. (Wing G9. —Dedication signed D. G.)

UNSATISFIED LOVERS. The unsatisfied lovers. A new English novel. Sold by J. Partridge. (Wing U94A)

VALENTINE AND ORSON. The famous history of Valentine and Orson. Written [i.e. abridged] by Laurence Price. For M. W., sold by D. Newman and B. Alsop. (Wing P3362. Second edition.)

ZAYAS Y SOTOMAYOR, MARIA DE. The perplex'd princess, or The famous novel of Donna Zagas. Written originally in Spanish. Tome I. For T. Malthus. (Esdaile)

1684

AMOROUS ABBESS. The amorous abbess: or Love in a nunnery. A novel. Translated from the French by a woman of quality. For R. Bentley. (Wing A3017 and B4343)

BEHN, APHRA. The adventures of the black lady. (Cited by Esdaile, without imprint, from the *DNB*. —This date probably is that of composition merely; first known edition is in the 1697 *Histories and novels*.)

BEHN, APHRA. Love-letters between a noble-man and his sister. R. Taylor. (Wing B1740. Second edition.)

BELLON, PETER. The amours of Bonne Sforza, Queen of Polonia. T. M. for R. Bently. (Wing B1849)

BOCCACCIO, GIOVANNI. The novels and tales of the renowned John Boccacio. The fifth edition. For A. Churchill. (Wing B3378. Fifth edition.)

BREMOND, GABRIEL DE. The pilgrim. Translated into English by P. Belon: Gent. For R. Bentley and M. Magnes. (Wing B4353A. Second edition. —Does not contain Bellon's continuation or sequel.)

64

BUNYAN, JOHN. The holy war. The second edition. For D. Newman; and B. Alsop. (Wing B5539. Second edition. —Some copies omit Alsop's name from title-page.)

BUNYAN, JOHN. The pilgrim's progress. The ninth edition. For N. Ponder. (Wing B5570. Fourteenth edition.)

BUNYAN, JOHN. The pilgrim's progress. The second part. For N. Ponder. (Wing B5576. First edition of this part.)

CHARLETON, WALTER. The Cimmerian matron. By P. M. Gent. For H. Herringman, sold by J. Knight and F. Saunders. (Wing C3667A. Third edition of this part.)

DELONEY, THOMAS. A most delectable history of the famous clothier of England, called Jack of Newbery. Written by W.S. H. B. for W. Thackeray. (Wing D958. —An abridgment.)

DUNTON, JOHN. The pilgrim's guide from the cradle to his death-bed. For J. Dunton. (Wing D2632)

EROTOPOLIS. Erotopolis. The present state of Betty-Land. For T. Fox. (Wing E3242)

EVE REVIVED. Eve revived, or The fair one stark naked. By W. Downing. (Wing E3175. —Translated from the French. —Probably same as the edition cited by Esdaile from the Term Catalogues.)

FORDE, EMANUEL. The most famous, delectable, and pleasant history of Parismus. The twelfth impression. M. H. and J. M. for J. Wright, J. Clarke, W. Thackeray, and T. Passinger. 2v. (Wing F5137. Sixteenth edition.)

FRENCH COURT. The history of the amours of the French court. Translated from the French. Obedience [i.e. London]: For N. B. [i.e. Newman and Bentley?]. (Wing H2143A. —Made up putting together *The history of the amours of the French court*, Newman 1684, and *Loves empire*, Bentley, 1682.)

FROST. An historical account of the late great frost in which are discovered, in several comical relations, the various humours, loves, cheats, and intreagues, of the town. For D. Brown and J. Walthoe. (Wing H2096)

GERMAN PRINCESS. The German Princess revived; or The London jilt; being a true account of the life and death of Jenny Voss. [Colophon] By G. Croom. (Wing G613)

GREENE, ROBERT. The pleasant history of Dorastus and Fawnia. H. Brugis for J. Clark, W. Thackeray and T. Passinger. (Wing G1836A. Sixteenth edition.)

HALL, JOSEPH. The travels of Don Francisco de Quevedo. A novel. For W. Grantham. (Wing Q195. —Another edition of Hall's *Discovery of a new world* [1609?].)

HEAD, RICHARD. The life and death of Mother Shipton. For B. Harris. (Wing H1258. Third edition.)

HOWARD, THOMAS. The history of the seven wise mistresses of Rome. For D. Newman. (Esdaile. Second edition.)

KEACH, BENJAMIN. The progress of sin; or The travels of Ungodliness. For J. Dunton. (Wing K80. First edition.)

KEACH, BENJAMIN. The travels of True Godliness. The third edition.

For J. Dunton. (Wing K98. Third edition; no second edition known.)

KEACH, BENJAMIN. The travels of True Godliness. The fifth edition. For J. Dunton. (Wing K99. Fifth edition; no fourth edition known.)

KEACH, BENJAMIN. The travels of True Godliness. The sixth edition. For J. Dunton. (Wing K99A. Sixth edition.)

LA ROBERDIERE. sieur de. Love victorious or The adventures of Oronces and Eugenia. Translated by J. E. For R. Bentley and S. Magnes. (Wing L445C. —Esdaile gives date of 1685, with no location.)

LEFEVRE, RAOUL. The destruction of Troy. The eleventh edition. For T. Passinger. (Wing L933. Thirteenth edition.)

LUCIAN. Lucian's Works, translated from the Greek. The first [-third] volume[s]. H. Clark for W. Benbridge. (Wing L3424. —Imprint varies slightly. —Volume 4-5 appeared in 1685.)

MALORY, Sir THOMAS. Brittains glory: or, The history of the life and death of K. Arthur. H. B. for J. Wright, J. Clark, W. Thackeray, and T. Passinger. (Wing M339. First edition of this abridgment. —Preface signed J. S., i.e. John Shirley?)

MANDEVILLE, Sir JOHN. The voyages and travels of Sir John Mandevile knight. For R. Scot, T. Basset, J. Wright, and R. Chiswel. (Wing M416. Seventeenth edition.)

MORE, Sir THOMAS. Utopia. Translated into English [by Gilbert Burnet]. For R. Chiswell. (Wing M2691. First edition of this translation.)

OLDYS, ALEXANDER. The London jilt: or, The politick whore. The second edition corrected. For H. Rodes. (Esdaile. Second edition.)

PLEASANT COMPANION. The pleasant companion, or Tryall of wits. By J. Grantham, for D. Brown, and J. Walthoe. (Wing P2539)

PRICE, LAURENCE. The witch of the woodlands. J. Millet, sold by J. Gilbertson. [ca.1684?] (Wing P3392. Fourth edition.)

REYNARD THE FOX. The shifts of Reynardine the son of Reynard the Fox. T. J. for E. Brewster. (Wing S3436. First appearance of this part.)

S., T. The second part of the Pilgrims progress. Edinburgh: The heir of A. Anderson. (Wing S181. Third edition. —Not by Bunyan.)

S., T. The second part of the Pilgrims progress. The second edition, with additions. G. Larkin, for T. Malthus. (Wing S180. Fourth edition. —Not by Bunyan.)

SEVEN SAGES. Erastus, or The Roman prince; being a more full account of the famous history of the seven wise masters. For D. Newman and B. Alsop. (Wing E3219. First appearance of this version.)

SEVEN SAGES. The history of the seven wise masters of Rome. For J. Wright. (Wing H2184. Eleventh edition.)

TRIUMPH OF FRIENDSHIP. The triumph of friendship, and The force of love. Two new novels from the French. For D. Brown and J. Walthoe. (Wing T2289A. —By Préchac?)

TOM TRAM. Tom Tram of the West, son-in-law to Mother Winter. For W. T., sold by J. Gilbertson. [ca. 1684] (Esdaile. First edition.)

66

YORKSHIRE ROGUE. The York-shire rogue, or Captain Hind improved. (Cited by Esdaile, without imprint, from Lowndes.)

1685

AMADIS DE GAULE. The history of Amadis de Gaul. For T. Passinger. (Cited by Esdaile from Passinger's list in *Valentine and Orson*, 1685. —An abridgment?)

BACON, Sir FRANCIS. New Atlantis. (In: Sylva sylvarum. The eleventh edition. J. Haviland, for W. Lee, sold by J. Williams. Wing B336. Third reissue of the 1676 edition.)

BACON, Sir FRANCIS. New Atlantis. (In: Sylva sylvarum. The eleventh edition For B. Griffin, sold by D. Brown and R. Sare. Wing B335. Thirteenth edition.)

BEHN, APHRA. Love-letters from a noble-man to his sister. The second part. For the author. (Pickering & Chatto 347:32. First appearance of this part.)

BREMOND, GABRIEL DE. The happy slave. In three parts compleat. The second edition. For G. Cownley. (Wing B4349. Third edition.)

BUNYAN, JOHN. The life and death of Mr. Badman. The second edition. For N. Ponder. (Wing B5551. Second edition.)

BUNYAN, JOHN. The pilgrim's progress. The tenth edition. For N. Ponder. (Wing B5571. Fifteenth edition.)

COURTILZ DE SANDRAS, GATIEN. The amorous conquests of the great Alcander. For R. Bentley, and S. Magnes. (Wing A3018)

CROUCH, NATHANIEL. The extra-ordinary adventures and discoveries of several famous men. By R. B. The second edition. For N. Crouch. (Wing C7324. Second edition.)

CROUCH, NATHANIEL. The surprizing miracles of nature and art. The second edition. By R. B. For N. Crouch. (Wing C7350. Second edition.)

CROUCH, NATHANIEL. Unparallel'd varieties. By R. B. The second edition. For N. Crouch. (Wing C7353. Second edition.)

CROUCH, NATHANIEL. Wonderful prodigies of judgment and mercy, discovered in above three hundred memorable histories. By R. B. For N. Crouch. (Wing C7361A. Third edition.)

DANGERFIELD, THOMAS. Dangerfield's Memoires, digested into adventures, receits, and expences. J. Bennet, for C. Brome. (Wing D190)

DELIGHTFUL NOVELS. Delightful and ingenious novels. For B. Crayle. (Wing D902. First edition. —Attributed by Crayle to John Reynolds.)

DELIGHTFUL NOVELS. Delightful and ingenious novels. The second edition. For B. Crayle. (Esdaile. Second edition.)

DELONEY, THOMAS. The first part of the pleasant and princely history of the gentle craft. J. Millet. for W. T., sold by J. Gilbertson. (Wing D945. Fifteenth edition.)

DUNTON, JOHN. An hue and cry after conscience: or The pilgrim's progress by candle-light. For J. Dunton. (Wing D2628)

FAUST. The history of the wicked life and damnable death of Dr. John

Faustus. For T. Passinger. [ca.1685] (Esdaile. First appearance of this abridgment.)

FAUST. The second report of Doctor John Faustus. For J. Conyers. (Cited by Esdaile from Conyers' list. Fifth edition.)

FORTUNATUS. The most excellent and delightful history of Fortunatus. A. M. for J. Conyers and J. Blare. [ca.1685] (Esdaile. An abridgment.)

GUY OF WARWICK. The renowned history, of the life and death of Guy Earl of Warwick. For P. Brooksby. (Wing S3516. Second edition of this version. —Preface signed John Shurley.)

KEACH, BENJAMIN. The progress of sin; or The travels of Ungodliness. The second edition. For J. Dunton. (Wing K81. Second edition.)

LETI, GREGORIO. The amours of Charles Duke of Mantua and Margaret Countess of Rovera. A novel. Translated out of Itallian. For H. Herringman, sold by J. Knight and F. Saunders. (Folger Library. Second edition.)

LE VAYER DE BOUTIGNY, ROLLAND. The famous romance of Tarsis and Zelie. Done into English by Charles Williams, Gent. For N. Ponder. (Wing L1797)

LUCIAN. Lucian's Works, translated from the Greek. The fourth [-fifth] volume[s]. For T. M., sold by J. Walthoe. (Wing L3424. —Volumes 1-3 appeared in 1684.)

MORE, Sir THOMAS. Utopia. Translated into English [by Gilbert Burnet]. For R. Chiswell, sold by G. Powell. (Wing M2692. Second edition of this translation.)

NICEROTUS. The history of Nicerotis, a pleasant novel. For R. Bentley and S. Magnes. (Wing H2128. —Esdaile cites also a fragment of another edition.)

PALLADINE. The excellent history of Palladine of England. For T. Passinger. [1685?] (Cited by Esdaile from Passinger's list in *Valentine and Orson*, 1685. Third edition.)

PALLADINE. The excellent history of Palladine of England. For E. Tracy. [1685?] (Cited by Esdaile from Tracy's list in *Valentine and Orson*, 1685. —An abridgment?)

PALMERIN OF ENGLAND. The famous history of the life of the renowned Prince Palmerin of England. In three parts. Now faithfully done into English. By J. S. For W. Thackeray. (Wing H3796. —An abridgment. —By John Shirley?)

PATRICK, Saint. The delightful history of the life and death of that renowned & famous St. Patrick. For D. Newman. (Wing D903)

POISSON, RAYMOND. The gallant ladies, or, The mutual confidence. A novel. For R. Baldwin. 2v. (Wing P2745, P2746. First edition.)

POISSON, RAYMOND. The galants: or, The reciprocal confidents. For J. Knight and F. Saunders. 2v. (Wing P2746A. Second edition of the above.)

PRECHAC, JEAN DE. The chaste seraglian: or, Yolanda of Sicily. A novel. Done out of French by T[homas] H[ayes] Gent. For R. Bentley and S. Magnes. (Wing P3204)

PRECHAC, JEAN DE. The grand vizier: or The history of the life of Cara Mustapha. H. Hills, jun. for J. Whitlock. (Wing P3205. First edition.)

PRECHAC, JEAN DE. The true history of Cara Mustapha. Now translated into English by Francis Philon. Gent. For L. Curtiss and H. Rodes. (Wing P3209. Another edition of the above.)

PRECHAC, JEAN DE. The Serasquior Bassa. An historical novel of the times. Done out of French. For H. Rodes. (Wing P3208A)

REYNARD THE FOX. The most pleasant history of Reynard the Fox. For J. Conyers, sold by J. Blare. [ca. 1685] (Esdaile. —An abridgment of part 1.)

REYNOLDS, JOHN. The glory of God's revenge against the bloody and detestable sins of murther and adultery. By Thomas Wright. T. Moore, for B. Crayle. (Wing W3708. First appearance of this abridgment. —Esdaile cites as imprint: For B. Crayle. [Wing R1308].)

ROBIN HOOD. The noble birth and gallant atchievements of . . . Robin Hood. M. Haly and J. Millet for J. Deacon. (Wing N1203. Third edition.)

STITCH, TOM. Wanton Tom: or, The merry history of Tom Stitch the taylor. For R. Barber. sold by R. Kell. (Wing W716)

THREE EXCELLENT NEW NOVELS. Three excellent new novels, containing many pleasant and delightful histories. For W. Whitwood. (Wing T1088. Third edition? —Cited by Esdaile as another edition of *The fortunate . . . lovers*, 1632 and 1683.)

VALENTINE AND ORSON. Valentine and Orson, the two sons of the Emperour of Greece. J. R. for T. Passinger. (Wing V30. Twelfth edition.)

ABU BAKR IBN AL-TUFAIL, ABU JAFAR. The history of Hai Eb'n Yockdan, an Indian prince. For R. Chiswell and W. Thorp. (Wing A151. —Translated by George Ashwell from Pocock's Latin version of the Arabic original. —A different version from that of 1674.)

ADELAIDE. Adellaide, a famed romance. In four parts. Bentley and Magnes. (Cited by Esdaile from Bentley and Magnes' advertisement.)

ALCOFORADO, M A R I A N N A D'. Five love-letters from a nun to a cavalier. Done out of French into English. By Sir Roger L'Estrange. For R. Bentley, sold by S. Cownley. (Wing A891. Third edition.)

BLACK TOM. The unlucky citizen: or, A pleasant history of the life of Black Tom. J. M. for J. Blare. (Wing U85)

BLIND BEGGAR. The history of the blind beggar of Bethnal-green. For C. Dennisson. (Wing H2146. Third edition.)

BONNECORSE, BALTHAZAR DE. La montre: or The lover's watch. R. H. for W. Canning. (Wing B3595C. —Translated by Aphra Behn. —See also 1688.)

BUNYAN, J O H N. The pilgrim's progress. The second part. The second edition. For N. Ponder. (Wing B5578. Second edition.)

CASTRO, HENRIQUEZ DE. Don Henriquez de Castro. Or, The conquest of the Indies. A Spanish novel. Translated . . . by a person of honour. R. E. for R. Bentley and S. Magnes. [1686] (Wing D1844)

CERVANTES SAAVEDRA, MIGUEL DE. The famous history of Don Quixote de la Mancha. For G. Conyers. (Wing C1772. —An abridgment.)

CHARACTER OF LOVE. The character of love, guided by inclination. Translated out of French. For R. Bentley. (Wing C2020. First edition.)

COURTILZ DE SANDRAS, GATIEN. The History of . . . that gallant Captain, Viscount de Turenne. By J. B. for D. Newman & R. Bentley. (Wing C6598 and D2414.)

DELIGHTFUL NOVELS. Delightful and ingenious novels. The third impression. For B. Crayle. (Esdaile. Third edition.)

DELIGHTFUL NOVELS. Delightful novels. Exemplifyed in eight choice and elegant histories. The fourth impression. For B. Crayle. (Wing D904. Fourth edition.)

GRISELDA. The pleasant and sweet history of Patient Grissell. For J. Clarke, W. Thackery, and T. Passinger. (Wing P2532. Mixed prose and verse; second edition of this version.)

GUY OF WARWICK. The famous history of Guy Earl of Warwick. By Samuel Smithson. For J. Clark, W. Thackeray, and T. Passinger. (Wing F376. Second edition of this version.)

HEAD, RICHARD. Nugae venales: or, A complaisant companion. The third edition. For E. Poole. (Wing H1267. Third edition.)

HELIODORUS. The Æthiopian history. The first five [books] translated by a person of quality, the last five by N. Tate. J. L. for E. Poole.

(Wing H1373. First edition of this version.)

HOWARD, THOMAS. The history of the seven wise mistresses of Rome. For M. Wotton, and G. Conyers. (Wing H3009. Third edition.)

JOHNSON, RICHARD. The famous history of the seven champions of Christendom. 3v. (Cited by Esdaile, without imprint, from Hazlitt. Thirtenth edition. —The third part, which appears here for the first time, has imprint: J. R. for B. Harris; and dedication signed W. W. [Wing J806].)

LOVE'S POSY. Love's posie: or, A collection of seven and twenty love letters, both in verse and prose. For J. Hindmarsh. (Wing L3281)

MERRY COMPANION. The merry companion, or The second part of the 'Antidote against melancholly'; . . . To which is added, histories, tales, and novels. For H. Playford. (Term Catalogues, II, 168)

MONTFORT, FRANÇOIS SALVAT, sieur de. The politick and heroick vertues of love display'd. Rendered out of French into English. Printed in the year. (Wing M2496A. —A reissue of the 1675 edition (*The Circle*).)

ORTGUE, PIERRE D', sieur de Vaumorière. Agiatis, Queen of Sparta. R.E. for R. Bentley and S. Magnes. (Wing V161)

PRECHAC, JEAN DE. The illustrious lovers, or Princely adventures in the courts of England and France. Now done into English. For W. Whitwood. (Wing I51. Second edition; first edition appeared under title of *The English princess*, 1678.)

PRECHAC, JEAN DE. The amours of Count Teckeli and the Lady Aurora Veronica de Serini. For R. Bentley and S. Magnes. (Wing P3203)

REYNOLDS, JOHN. The glory of God's revenge against . . . murther and adultery. By Thomas Wright. T. Moore for B. Crayle. (Wing W3709. Second edition of this abridgment.)

SHIPTON, URSULA. The strange and wonderful history of Mother Shipton. For W. H., sold by J. Conyers. (Wing S5848. —Esdaile cites also, without imprint, another version, with title: *The history of Mother Shipton.*)

1687

BEHN, APHRA. The amours of Philander and Silvia: being the third and last part of the Love-letters between a noble-man and his sister. Sold by most book-sellers. (Wing B1741. First appearance of this part.)

BOYLE, ROBERT. The martyrdom of Theodora, and of Didymus. H. Clark, for J. Taylor and C. Skegnes. (Wing B3987)

BUNYAN, JOHN. The pilgrim's progress. The second part. For N. Ponder. (Wing B5579. Third edition.)

CARTIGNY, JEAN DE. The conviction of worldly-vanity: or, The wandring prodigal, and his return. G. L. for J. Harris. (Wing S50. —Dedication signed: J. S. [i.e. John Shirley?])

CERVANTES SAAVEDRA, MIGUEL DE. The history of the most renowned Don Quixote of Mancha. Now made English according to the humour of our modern language. By J. P[hilips]. T. Hodgkin, sold by J. Newton. (Wing C1774A. First edition of this translation. —Some copies have variant imprint: Sold by W. Whitwood. Wing C1774.)

CHAUCER, junior, pseud. Canterbury tales: composed for the entertainment of all ingenuous young men and maids. For J. Back. (Wing C3737)

CHAVIGNY DE LA BRETONNIERE, FRANÇOIS DE. The gallant hermaphrodite. An amorous novel. For S. Manship. (Wing C3757A. First edition.)

CHILDREN IN THE WOOD. The history of the children in the wood. I. M. for J. Blare. (Wing H2147. First edition.)

CROUCH, NATHANIEL. The history of the nine worthies of the world. By R. B. For N. Crouch. (Wing C7337. First edition.)

CYNTHIA. Cynthia; with the tragical account of the unfortunate loves of Almerin and Desdemona. A novel. R. Holt, for T. Passinger, and R. Fenner, Canterbury. (Wing C7710A. First edition.)

CYRANO DE BERGERAC, HERCULE SAVINIEN DE. The comical history of the states and empires of the worlds of the moon and sun. Newly Englished by A. Lovell, A. M. For H. Rhodes. (Wing C7717. —Another version had appeared in 1659.)

FAUST. The historie of the damnable life and deserved death of Doctor John Faustus. For W. Whitwood. [1687?] (Wing H2154. Tenth edition.)

FAUST. The second report for Doctor John Faustus. For W. Whitwood. [1687?] (Esdaile. Sixth edition.)

FORDE, EMANUEL. The famous history of Montelion. J. R. and W. W. for W. Thackeray, and T. Passenger. (Wing F1529. Tenth edition.)

GIBBS, RICHARD. The new disorders of love. A gallant novel. For R. Bentley and S. Magnes. (Wing G666)

HEAD, RICHARD. The life and death of Mother Shipton. For W. Harris. (Wing H1259. Fourth edition.)

HEAD, RICHARD. Nugae venales: or, A complaisant companion. The fourth edition. For E. Poole. (Term Catalogues. Fourth edition.)

HELIODORUS. The t r i u m p h s of love and constancy. The first five [books] rendred by a person of quality, the last five by N. Tate. The second edition. J. Leake, for E. Poole. (Wing H1374. Second edition; first appeared in 1686 as The Æthiopian history.)

JOHNSON, RICHARD. The famous history of the seven champions of Christendom. For R. Scot, T. Basset, R. Chiswell, M. Wotton, and G. Conyers. 2v. (Wing J799. Fourteenth edition. —Pt. 3 appeared the preceding year.)

LA CALPRENEDE, GAUTIER DE COSTES, sieur de. Hymen's praeludia; or, Love's master-piece. Elegantly rendred into English, by Robert Loveday. F. Collins for T. Fabian. (Wing L124. Fifth edition.)

OTTOMAN GALLANTRIES. Ottoman gallantries: or The life of the Bassa of Buda. Done out of French [by B. Berenclow]. For R. Bentley and S. Magnes. (Wing O536)

PATRICK SIMON. The parable of the pilgrim. The sixth edition. For R. Chiswell. (Wing P832. Seventh edition.)

REYNOLDS, JOHN. The glory of God's revenge against . . . murther and adultery. For B. Crayle. (Cited by Esdaile, with question mark, from the Term Catalogues. Third edition.)

SEVEN SAGES. The history of the seven wise masters of Rome. For M. Wotton and G. Conyers. (Wing H2185. Twelfth edition.)

SPANISH DECAMERON. The Spanish decameron: or, Ten novels. Made English by R[oger] L[Estrange]. For S. Neale. (Wing C1780. —The stories are taken from Cervantes and Solórzano.)

WINSTANLEY, WILLIAM. The honour of the taylors: or, The famous and renowned history of Sir John Hawkwood, Knight. W. Whitwood. (Wing H2599. —Cf. also 1668.)

1688

BEHN, APHRA. The fair jilt: or, The history of Prince Tarquin and Miranda. R. Holt, for W. Canning. (Wing B1729. —Caption title: The fair hypocrite.)

BEHN, APHRA. Oroonoko: or, The royal slave. A true history. For W. Canning. (Wing B1749)

BEHN, APHRA. T h r e e histories: Oroonoko, The fair jilt, and Agnes de Castro. For W. Canning. (Wing B1766A. First edition of this collection. —Each title also issued separately.)

BLACKBOURN, RICHARD. Clitie, a novel. For R. Bentley and S. Magnes. (Wing B3066)

BLACKBOURN, RICHARD. Three novels in one, viz: The constant lovers, The fruits of jealousie, and Wit in a woman. Together with Sempronia or The unfortunate mother. For G. Grafton. (Esdaile.)

BONNECORSE, BALTHAZAR DE. The art of making love without speaking. For R. Bentley. (Wing A3793. —Translated by Peter Bellon. —Appeared also in *Two new novels*, 1688.)

BRILLAC, J   B   DE. The fatal beauty of Agnes de Castro. For W. Canning. (Wing B4693A. —Appeared also in *Two new novels*, 1688, and in Behn's *Three histories*, 1688.)

BUNYAN, JOHN. The life and death of Mr. Badman. The second edition. For N. Ponder. (Wing B5552. Third edition.)

BUNYAN, JOHN. The pilgrim's progress. The eleventh edition. For N. Ponder. (Wing B5572. Sixteenth edition.)

CHAVIGNY DE LA BRETONNIERE, FRANÇOIS DE. The gallant hermaphrodite. For S. Manship. (Wing C3757B. Second edition.)

CLAUDE, ISAAC. The Count d'Soissons. A gallant novel. Translated out of French. J. B. for R. Bentley and S. Magnes. (Wing C4586)

CROUCH, NATHANIEL. F e m a l e excellency, or The ladies glory. By R. B. For N. Crouch. (Wing C7326)

DU VIGNAN,   , sieur. The Turkish secretary. With the circumstances of a Turkish adventure. J. B., sold by J. Hindmarsh and R. Taylor. (Wing D2922)

FORDE, EMANUEL. The famous, pleasant, and delightful history of Ornatus and Artesia. For G. Conyers. [1688?] (Esdaile. First edition of this abridgment.)

GREENE, ROBERT. The pleasant history of Dorastus and Fawnia. For G. Conyers. (Wing G1837. Seventeenth edition.)

HEAD, RICHARD. The E n g l i s h rogue, containing a brief discovery of the most eminent cheats . . . by him committed. For J. Blare. (Wing H1245. Second edition of this abridgment of part 1.)

HEAD, RICHARD. The E n g l i s h rogue. The four parts. To which is added a fifth part. For J. Back. (Wing H1252. First edition of this abridgment. —Preface signed M. L.)

HOWARD, THOMAS. The history of the seven wise mistresses of Rome. (Cited by Esdaile, without imprint, from Hazlitt. Fourth edition.)

LA FAYETTE, MARIE MADELEINE, comtesse de. The Princess of Cleves. For R. Bentley and S. Magnes. (Wing L170. Second edition.)

LAZARILLO DE TORMES. The pleasant adventures of the witty Spaniard, Lazarillo de Tormes. To which is added, The life and death of Young Lazarillo. J. Leake. (Wing P2529. First edition of this version.)

PENTON, STEPHEN. The guardian's instruction, or, The gentleman's romance. For the author, sold by S. Miller. (Wing P1439)

PHILLIPS, WILLIAM. A new fairing for the merrily disposed, or The comical history of the famous merry andrew, W. Phill———. For H. Wallis. (Wing P2117)

73

PLEASURES OF MATRIMONY.
The pleasures of matrimony, inter-mix'd with variety of merry and delightful stories. A. G. for H. Rhodes. (Wing P2565. First edition.)

PRECHAC, JEAN DE. The disorders of Basset, a novel. Done out of French. For J. Newton. (Wing D1673)

REYNOLDS, JOHN. God's revenge against murther and adultery. By Thomas Wright. The second edition. For B. Crayle. (Wing W3710. Fourth edition. —Earlier editions appeared under title: *The glory of God's revenge. . . .*)

S., T. The history of the loves of Lysander and Sabina: a novel. J. Taylor. (Wing S165. —Said by Esdaile to be a second edition of *Lisander or The souldier of fortune*, 1681.)

SEVEN SAGES. The history of the seven wise masters of Rome. For M. Wotton, and G. Conyers. (Esdaile; Newberry Library. A re-issue of the twelfth edition.)

TALLEMANT, PAUL. Lycidus: or The lover in fashion. From the French. For J. Knight and F. Saunders. (Wing T129. —Dedication signed A. Behn.)

TWO NEW NOVELS. Two new novels. I. The art of making love [by B. de Bonnecorse.] II. The fatal beauty of Agnes de Castro [by J. B. de Brillac]. Translated from the French by P[eter] B[ellon] G[ent]. For R. Bentley. (Wing T3491. —Each story also appeared separately.)

VALENTINE AND ORSON. Valentine and Orson, the two sons of the Emperour of Greece. J. R. for T. Passenger. (Wing V31. Thirteenth edition.)

AESOP. Aesops Fables, English and Latin. By M. F. for the Company of Stationers. (Wing A704. Probably the first appearance of Hoole's version; the 30th of 40 editions of the fables in English during the period down to 1700.)

AESOP. Mythologica ethica, or Three centuries of Aesopian Fables. By Philip Ayres, Esq. For T. Hawkins. (Wing A731. First edition of this version; the 31st of 40 editions of the fables in English during the period down to 1700.)

ANNE, OF AUSTRIA. The amours of Ann (Queen to Lewis the 13th) with the Cavalier de Roan, the true father of the present Lewis the 14th. For A. Roper. (Term Catalogues, II, 287.)

BEHN, APHRA. The history of the nun, or The fair vow-breaker. For A. Baskerville. (Wing B1737)

BEHN, APHRA. The lucky mistake. For R. Bentley. (Wing B1745)

BELLON, PETER. The court secret. Written by P. B. Gent. R. E. for R. Bentley. 2 pts. (Wing B1850, B1851 —Part 2 has imprint: For R. Bentley and S. Magnes. —Some copies have variant imprint for part 1: R. E. for R. Baldwin.)

BERNARD, CATHERINE. The count of Amboise; or The generous lover. A novel. Rendred into English by P[eter] B[ellon] Gent. For R. Bentley and M. Magnes. (Wing B1983)

BEVIS OF HAMPTON. The famous and renowned history of Sir Bevis of Southampton. For W. Thackeray, and J. Deacon. (Wing F359. First edition. —Preface signed S. J.)

74

BUNYAN, JOHN. The pilgrim's progress. The twelfth edition. For R. Ponder. (New York Public Library. Seventeenth edition.)

CERVANTES SAAVEDRA, MIGUEL DE. The delightful history of Don Quixot. For B. Crayle. (Wing C1771. First edition of this abridgment.)

ELIZABETH, Queen. The secret history of the most renowned Q. Elizabeth and the E. of Essex. Cologne [London]: For Will with the wisp [i.e. R. Bentley]. (Wing S2344. Fourth edition.)

FORDE, EMANUEL. The most famous, delectable, and pleasant history of Parismus. The thirteenth impression. J. Millit, for W. Thackeray. 2v. (Wing F1538. Seventeenth edition.)

FORTUNATUS. The right, pleasant, and diverting history of Fortunatus. For J. Deacon. [1689?] (Cited by Esdaile from Deacon's list. —A different version?)

GESTA ROMANORUM. A record of ancient histories, entituled in Latin, Gesta Romanroum. For T. Basset, R. Chiswell, A. Mill, G. Conyers, and M. Wotton. (Wing R638. Twenty-first edition.)

HEAD, RICHARD. The English rogue. The four parts. To which is added a fifth part. The second edition. (Wing H1252A (without imprint). Second edition of this abridgment.)

INTRIGUES OF LOVE. The intrigues of love, or The amours and gallantries of the French court during the reign of . . . Henry IV. Newly made English from the French, by Sir Edwin Sadleir. Sold by B. Crayle. (Esdaile. —Cf. also 1682.)

JOHNSON, RICHARD. The famous history of the seven champions of Christendom. The third part. W. Thackeray. (Cited by Esdaile from an advertisement of Thackeray's.)

MESSALINA. The amours of Messalina, late Queen of Albion. For J. Lyford. 2v. (Wing A3023. —By Gregorio Leti?— Part 2 has title: *The Royal wanton*, and imprint: For J. B. [Wing R2158].)

MESSALINA. Love letters betwen Polydorus, the Gothick king, and Messalina, late Queen of Albion. Paris [i.e. London?]: For J. Lyford. (Harvard University Library. —Same as part 2 of *The amours of Messalina*, above.)

PEPPA. Peppa: or, The reward of constant love. A novel. Done out of French . . . by a young gentlewoman. For W. Crooke. (Wing P1448. —Dedication signed A. C.)

PLEASURES OF MATRIMONY. The pleasures of matrimony, intermix'd with variety of merry and delightful stories. The second edition. For H. Rhodes. (Term Catalogues, II, 294. Second edition.)

QUEVEDO Y VILLEGAS, FRANCISCO DE. Visions. Made English by R[oger] L[Estrange]. The seventh edition corrected. For H. Herringman, sold by F. Saunders. (Wing Q201. Ninth edition.)

RIVAL PRINCESSES. The rival princesses: or, The Colchian court: a novel. For R. Bentley. (Wing R1547)

SPANISH AND FRENCH HISTORY. The Spanish and French history: or, Love out of season. Out of French. For W. Hull. (Wing S4803)

SULTANA OF BARBARY. The amours of the Sultana of Barbary. A novel. In two parts. Sold by R. Baldwin. (Wing A3028. First edition.)

VIROTTO AND DOROTHEA. The governor of Cyprus, or The loves of Virotto and Dorothea. For J. Knapton. (Esdaile)

WANTON FRIAR. The wanton fryer, or The Irish amour. Sold by R. Baldwin. (Esdaile)

WINSTANLEY, WILLIAM. The honour of the taylors: or, The famous and renowned history of Sir John Hawkwood. W. T h a c k e r a y. (Esdaile. Second edition?)

1690

B., A. The merry tales of the madmen of Gotam. By J. R. for G. Conyers and J. Dacon. [1690?] (Wing B3749. Fifth edition. —Ascribed to Andrew Borde.)

BELLON, PETER. The reviv'd fugitive: a gallant historical novel. For R. Bentley. (Wing B1858)

BIONDI, GIOVANNI FRANCISCO. Love and revenge. An excellent romance. Englished by James Hayward. The second edition. For W. Miller. (Esdaile. Second edition; first edition as *Eromena, or, Love and revenge*.)

BEHN, APHRA. T h r e e histories: Oroonoko, The fair jilt, and Agnes de Castro. T. Walthroe. (Esdaile. Second edition? —Each title was advertised separately by Walthoe.)

BUNYAN, J O H N. The pilgrim's progress. The second part. The third edition. For R. Ponder. (Wing B5580. Fourth edition.)

CABINET OPENED. The cabinet open'd, or The secret history of the amours of Madam de Maintenon, with the French king. Translated from the French copy. For R. Baldwin. (Wing C190)

CHEVY-CHASE. The famous and renowned history of the memorable but unhappy hunting on Chevy-Chase. By and for C. Brown. [ca. 1690] (C. A. Stonehill 149)

COX, H. Lisarda; or The travels of love and jealousy. A novel. In two parts. By H. C. Gent. For J. Knight. (Newberry Library)

DELONEY, THOMAS. The pleasant and princely history of the gentle craft. For H. Rhodes. [ca.1690] 48p. (Wing D961. Sixteenth edition. —Esdaile also cites a 51p. edition with same imprint, also undated (seventeenth edition), and another, mutilated, at the British Museum, without imprint, arbitrarily dated by being placed here (eighteenth edition).)

DELONEY, T H O M A S. The shoemakers glory: or, The princely history of the gentle craft. C. Brown. [ca.1690] (Esdaile. First edition of this version.)

DELONEY, THOMAS. The pleasant history of John Winchcomb in his younger years called Jack of Newbery. Now the fourteenth time imprinted. W. Wilde, for T. Passenger and W. Thackeray. [ca.1690] (Wing D964. Fifteenth edition.)

DELONEY, THOMAS. Thomas of Reading. Sold by J. Deacon. [ca.1690] (Esdaile. Ninth edition.)

DELONEY, THOMAS. The honour of the cloathworking trade: or, . . . Thomas of Reading. For J. Deacon. [ca.1690?] (Esdaile. —An abridgment.)

FAUST. The history of the damnable life and deserved death of Doctor John Faustus. For W. Whitwood, sold by T. Sawbridge. (Esdaile. Eleventh edition.)

FAUST. The history of the wicked life and damnable death of Dr. John Faustus. For C. Dennisson. [ca.1690] (Cited by Esdaile, with question mark, from advertisement. Second edition of this abridgment.)

FRANK, JOHN. The birth, life and death of John Frank. J. M. for J. Deacon and C. Dennisson. [ca.1690] (Esdaile. —There is also another undated edition cited in Esdaile, with imprint: J. M. for J. Deacon.)

G., J. The city revels, or, The humours of Bartholomew-Fair. Sold by R. Taylor. (Hazlitt (who gives author as T. C.). The Term Catalogues, II, 334, give the publishers as T. Howkins and J. Harris.)

GALLANTRY UNMASKED. Gallantry unmasked, or Women in their proper colours. A novel. For B. R., sold by R. Baldwin. (Wing G176A)

GREENE, ROBERT. The pleasant history of Dorastus and Fawnia. J. W. for G. Conyers. [ca.1690?] (Wing G1838. Eighteenth edition.)

GREENE, ROBERT. The delightful history of Doratus and Fawnia. [ca.1690] For C. Dennisson. (Esdaile. An abridgment.)

HENRY VIII. The pleasant and delightful history of King Henry 8th and a cobler. For C. Dennisson. [ca.1690] (Wing P2530. Second edition.)

HENRY VIII. The pleasant and delightful history of King Henry the VIII. and the Abbot of Reading. J. M. for C. Dennisson. [ca.1690] (Esdaile)

HERO AND LEANDER. The famous and renowned history of the two unfortunate, tho noble, lovers, Hero and Leander. A. Milbourn, for J. Blare. [ca.1690] (Huntington Library. —Preface signed J. S. —Wing F361 with imprint Newcastle: J. White, is probably eighteenth century.)

HIND, JAMES. No jest like a true jest. For J. Deacon [ca.1690?] (Wing N1177. —Fourth edition.)

IRISH ROGUE. The Irish rogue, or The comical history of . . . Teague O'Divelley. For G. Conyers. [1690] (Wing I1045)

LADLE, TOM. The pleasant history of Tom Ladle. For J. Blare. [ca.1690] (Esdaile. —Another edition was advertised by C. Dennisson.)

LA FAYETTE, MARIE MADELEINE, comtesse de. Zayde. A Spanish history, or, romance. Originally written in French. By Monsieur Segray. Done into English by P. Porter. The second edition. For F. Saunders. (Wing L173. Second edition.)

LA FERTE SENNETERRE, La Mareschalesse de. History of the Mareschalesse de la Ferté. (In: Gallantry unmasked. For B. R., sold by R. Baldwin. Wing G176A. —This section has its own title-page [Wing H2169].)

LA ROCHE GUILHEM, Mlle de. The great Scanderbeg. A novel. For R. Bentley. (Wing C3801. —Also attributed to Urbain Chevreau. —Dedication signed N. V.)

MAZARIN, HORTENSE (MANCINI) DE LA PORTE, duchesse de. The memoires of the Dutchess Mazarine. Done into English by P. Porter. The third impression. For R. Bentley. (Wing S356. Third edition. —Sometimes attributed to the Abbé de Saint Réal.)

MESSALINA. The royal wanton: containing the Gallick intrigues . . . Being the second part of the Amours of Messalina . . . For F. B. (British Museum. A re-issue of the 1689 edition.)

MORGAN, SCHON AP. The wonderful adventures and happy success of young Schon ap Morgan, the only son of Sheffery ap Morgan. For J. Deacon. [ca.1690?] (Esdaile)

MORGAN, SHEFFERY AP. The life and death of Sheffery ap Morgan. For J. Deacon. [ca.1690?] (Esdaile, who lists two editions, both undated, with same imprint.)

PAGAN PRINCE. The pagan prince: or A comical history of the heroick atchievements of the Palatine of Eboracum. Amsterdam [L o n d o n]: (Wing P163)

PHILANTUS AND BELLAMOND. The amours of Philantus and Bellamond. For F. Saunders. (Wing A3024. First edition.)

PORTSMOUTH, L O U I S E KEROUAILLE, Duchess of. The secret history of the Dutchess of Portsmouth; giving an account of the intreagues of the court, during her ministry. For R. Baldwin. (Wing S2340)

REYNARD THE FOX. The most pleasing and delightful history of Reynard the Fox and Reynardine his son: in two parts. For J. Blare. [ca. 1690?] (Esdaile. First edition of this abridgment.)

ROBIN HOOD. The noble birth and gallant atchievements of . . . Robin Hood. J. M., sold by J. Deacon. [1690?] (Esdaile. Fourth edition.)

SCOGGIN, JOHN. Scogins jests: full of witty mirth, and pleasant shifts. Gathered by Andrew Board. For W. Thackeray, and J. Deacon. [1690?] (Wing B3750. Second edition of the 1626 text, slightly abridged.)

SHIRLEY, JOHN. The famous history of Aurelius, the valiant Londonprentice. For J. Back. [ca.1690?] (Esdaile. Second edition.)

TOM TRAM. Tom Tram of the west, son-in-law to Mother Winter. For W. T., sold by J. Deacon. [ca. 1690] (Esdaile. Second edition.)

TRUMBILL, . The Dutch whore; or, The miss of Amsterdam. (Esdaile, without imprint.)

WEAMYS, ANNE. A continuation of Sir Philip Sidney's Arcadia. The second edition. For W. Miller. (Esdaile. Second edition.)

WINSTANLEY, WILLIAM. The Essex champion: or, The famous history of Sir Billy of Billerecay. For J. Blare. [ca.1690] (Wing E3342. First edition.)

1691

ADOLPHUS. The history of Adolphus, Prince of Russia. By a person of quality. Sold by R. T. (Wing H2113. —Esdaile gives as imprint: Sold by R. S.)

AESOP. Aesops Fables, with their morals. The twelfth edition. For F. Eglesfield, sold by R. Taylor. (Unidentified version; the 32d of 40 editions of the fables in English in the period down to 1700.)

ANNE, OF AUSTRIA. The French king proved a bastard: or The amours of Anne (Queen to Louis XIII.) with the Chevalier de Roan. The second edition. For A. Roper.

AULNOY, MARIE CATHERINE JU-MELLE DE BERNEVILLE, comtesse d'. The ingenious and diverting letters of the Lady ———'s travels into Spain. For S. Crouch. (Term Catalogues. First edition. —Parts 1-2 only; part 3 appeared in 1692.)

BEVIS OF HAMPTON. The gallant history of the life and death of that most noble knight, Sir Bevis of Southampton. A. M. for J. Deacon. [1691?] (Wing G170. First edition of this version.)

CROUCH, NATHANIEL. Delightful fables in prose and verse, none of them to be found in Aesop. By R. B. For N. Crouch. (Wing C7311)

DUNTON, JOHN. A voyage round the world: . . . The rare adventures of Don Kainophilus. For R. Newcome. 3v. (Wing V742. —Volume 1 is undated.)

ELIZABETH, Queen. The secret history of the Duke of Alancon and Q. Elizabeth. For Will with the whisp [i.e. R. Bentley?] (Wing S2341)

PALMERIN OF ENGLAND. The famous history of the life of the renowned Prince Palmerin of England. In three parts. Now faithfully done into English . . . by J. S. For W. Thackeray and J. Back. (Esdaile. Second edition of this abridgment.)

SCUDERY, MADELEINE DE. Artamenes; or, The grand Cyrus. In ten parts. Englished by F. G. esq; For J. Darby, R. Roberts, B. Griffin, and R. Everingham. (Wing S2145. Second edition. —Parts 2-10 have separate title-page dated 1690.)

SIDNEY, Sir PHILIP. The most pleasant and delightful history of Argalus

and Parthenia. J. M. for E. Tracy, sold by J. Blare. (Wing Q109. Third edition.)

1692

AESOP. Fables, of Æsop and other eminent mythologists: with morals and reflexions. By Sir Roger L'Estrange, Kt. For R. Sare, T. Sawbridge, B. Took, M. Gillyflower, A. & J. Churchil, and J. Hindmarsh. (Wing A706. First edition of L'Estrange's version; the 33d of 40 editions of the fables in English during the period down to 1700.)

ARGENCES, D'. The Countess of Salisbury; or, The most noble order of the Garter. Done out of French by Mr. Ferrand Spence. For R. Bentley and S. Magnes. (Wing A3630A. Second edition.)

AULNOY, MARIE CATHERINE JU-MELLE DE BERNEVILLE, comtesse d'. The ingenious and diverting letters of the Lady ———. The second edition. For S. Crouch. 3v. (Wing B2038, B2040, B2041. —Second edition.)

AULNOY, MARIE CATHERINE JU-MELLE DE BERNEVILLE, comtesse d'. Memoirs of the court of France. R. Bentley and T. Bennett. (Wing A4318A. First edition.)

AULNOY, MARIE CATHERINE JU-MELLE DE BERNEVILLE, comtesse d'. Memoirs of the court of Spain. Done into English by T. Brown. For T. Horn, F. Saunders, and T. Bennet. (Wing A4220)

CHARACTER OF LOVE. The character of love, guided by inclination. Translated out of French. For R. Bentley. (Wing C2020A. Second edition.)

79

CONGREVE, WILLIAM. Incognita: or, Love and duty reconcil'd. For P. Buck. (Wing C5848. First edition.)

DANIEL, GABRIEL. A voyage to the world of Cartesius. Written originally in French, and now translated into English. T. Bennet. (Wing D201. First edition. —Second edition of 1694 bears translator's name, T. Taylor.)

GILDON, CHARLES. The post-boy rob'd of his mail: or, The pacquet broke open. For J. Dunton. (Wing G735A. —Part 1 only; part 2 appeared following year.)

LA ROCHE GUILHEM, Mlle de. Zingis: A Tartarian history. Written in Spanish, and Translated into English by J. M. For F. Saunders and R. Parker. (Wing L450)

OLDYS, ALEXANDER. The female gallant or, The wife's the cuckold. A novel. For S. Briscoe. (Wing O265)

REYNOLDS, JOHN. The garden of love, and royal flowers of fidelity: now much amplified by several hands. The fourth edition. For N. Boddington and J. Back. (Esdaile. —If this is Reynolds' Flower of fidelitie, it is the fifth edition.)

RIVAL MOTHER. The rival mother; a late true history: digested into a novel. For R. Baldwin. (Wing R1546)

SECRET LETTERS. The secret letters of amour between the Dutchess and mynheer. [Without imprint.] (Wing S2350)

SHIRLEY, JOHN. The famous history of the valiant London-prentice. (Wing S60 (without imprint). Third edition.)

SIEGE OF MENTZ. The siege of Mentz. Or, The German heroin, a novel. For S. Briscoe. (Wing S3771)

W., D. Taxila, or Love prefer'd before duty. A novel. For T. Salusbury. (Esdaile. —Another translation of La Roche Guilhem's *Zingis*. —Rolfe *PMLA*, XLIX [1934], 1083)

1693

ALCOFORADO, MARIANNA D'. Five love-letters from a nun to a cavalier. Done out of French into English, by Sir Roger L'Estrange. For R. Bentley. (Wing A892. Fourth edition.)

ALCOFORADO, MARIANNA D'. Seven Portuguese letters, being a second part to the Five love-letters from a nun to a cavalier. For C. Brome. (Wing A894. Second edition.)

AMADIS DE GAULE. The most excellent and famous history of the most renowned knight Amadis of Greece. For J. Deacon and J. Blare. (Wing M2877. —The seventh book of the Amadis series.)

AULNOY, MARIE CATHERINE JUMELLE DE BERNEVILLE, comtesse d'. The present court of Spain. For H. Rhodes and J. Harris. (Wing A4223)

BEHN, APHRA. Love letters between a noble-man and his sister. For J. Hindmarsh and J. Tonson. 3v. (Wing B1742. Third edition.)

BUNYAN, JOHN. The pilgrim's progress. The thirteenth edition. For R. Ponder, sold by N. Boddington. (Wing B5574. Eighteenth edition.)

BUNYAN, JOHN. The pilgrim's progress. The second part. The sixth edition. For R. Ponder. (Wing B5581. Sixth edition; no fifth edition known.)

BUNYAN, JOHN. The pilgrim's progress. The third part. E. Millet, for J. Deacon, J. Back, and J. Blare. (Wing B5583. First edition of this spurious continuation.)

COX, H. The travels of love and jealousie. A novel, in two parts. For R. Bentley and D. Brown. (Esdaile. Second edition: first edition, 1690, appeared under title: *Lisarda*.)

FOIGNY, GABRIEL DE. A new discovery of Terra incognita australis, or the southern world. By James Sadeur [pseud.]. Translated from the French copy. For J. Dunton. (Wing F1395)

GILDON, CHARLES. The second volume of The post-boy robb'd of his mail. For J. Dunton (?). (Wing G4. —Volume 1 appeared in 1692.)

HEAD, RICHARD. The English rogue. The four parts. To which is added a fifth part. The third edition. For J. Back. (Esdaile. Third edition of this abridgment.)

LAZARILLO DE TORMES. The pleasant adventures of the witty Spaniard, Lazarillo de Tormes. To which is added, The life and death of Young Lazarillo. For H. Rhodes. (Esdaile. Second edition of this version.)

PLAYER'S TRAGEDY. The player's tragedy. Or, Fatal love, a new novel. R. Taylor. (Wing P2418)

PLEASURES OF MATRIMONY. The pleasures of matrimony, intermix'd with variety of merry and delightful stories. The fourth edition. For H. Rhodes. (Esdaile. Fourth edition; no third edition known.)

RABELAIS, FRANÇOIS. The third book of the works of Mr. Francis Rabelais. Now faithfully translated into English by the unimitable pen of Sir Thomas Vrwhart. For R. Baldwin. (Wing R110. —First appearance of this book; books 1-2 appeared in 1653, books 4-5 in 1694.)

SEVEN SAGES. The history of the seven wise masters of Rome. Glasgow: R. Sanders. (Wing H2186. Thirteenth edition.)

VIRTUE REWARDED. Vertue rewarded; or, The Irish princess. A new novel. For R. Bentley. (Wing V647)

1694

AESOP. Fables, of Aesop and other eminent mythologists. By Sir Roger L'Estrange, Kt. The second edition. For R. Sare, B. Took, M. Gillyflower, A. & J. Churchill, J. Hindmarsh, and G. Sawbridge. (Wing A707. Second edition of this version; the 34th of 40 editions of the fables in English during the period down to 1700.)

AMADIS DE GAULE. The most excellent and famous history of the most renowned knight Amadis of Greece. For J. Deacon and J. Blare. (Wing (without number, follows M2877). A re-issue of the 1693 edition.)

BEHN, APHRA. Love-letters between a noble-man and his sister. For J. H. [and] J. T., sold by T. Bennet. (University of Pennsylvania Library. Re-issue of 1693 edition with cancel title.)

CERVANTES SAAVEDRA, MIGUEL DE. Select novels. Translated from the originals by Dr. Walter Pope. For C. Brome and T. Horne. (Wing C1779. First edition of this translation, which contains six of the *Exemplary novels*, together with *Patient Grisel*.)

CHAMILLY, NOEL BOUTON, marquis de. Five love-letters written by a cavalier, in answer to the five love-letters written to him by a nun. For R. Bentley. (Wing F1111. Second edition. —Caption title: The answers of the Chevalier Del.)

DANIEL, GABRIEL. A voyage to the world of Cartesius. Translated into English by T. Taylor. The second edition. For T. Bennet. (Wing D202. Second edition.)

FORDE, EMANUEL. The famous, pleasant, and delightful history of Ornatus and Artesia. For J. Deacon. [1694?] (Esdaile. Second edition of this abridgment.)

FRENCH ROGUE. The French rogue, or The life of Mon. Ragoue de Versailles. Done from the original by J. S. For N. Boddington. (Esdaile. A different version from that of 1672.)

GREENE, ROBERT. The pleasant history of Dorastus and Fawnia. (Cited by Esdaile, without imprint, from Hazlitt. Nineteenth edition.)

HEAD, RICHARD. The life and death of Mother Shipton. For J. Back. (Esdaile. Fifth edition.)

HELVETIAN HERO. The adventures of the Helvetian hero, with the young Countess of Albania; or, The amours of Armadorus and Vincentina: a novel. For R. Taylor. (Wing A605)

JOHNSON, RICHARD. The famous history of the seven champions of Christendom. The third part. J. Deacon. [ca.1694] (Cited by Esdaile from Deacon's advertisement. Third edition of this part.)

MACHIAVELLI, NICCOLO. The marriage of Belphegor. (In: The works of the famous Nicholas Machiavel. For R. Clavel, C. Harper, J. Robinson, J. Amery, A. and J. Churchil. Wing M130. Sixth edition.)

PENTON, STEPHEN. New instructions to the guardian. For W. Kettilby. (Wing P1440)

PETRONIUS ARBITER. The satyr of Titus Petronius Arbiter, a Roman knight. Made English by Mr. Burnaby of the Middle Temple, and another hand. For S. Briscoe. (Wing P1881)

PRESTON, RICHARD GRAHAM, Viscount. The moral state of England . . . With the life of Theodatus, and three novels. By the Lord P. For R. Bentley and D. Brown. (Wing P3313. Second edition. —Date on title-page reads 8694 instead of 1694.)

RABELAIS, FRANÇOIS. The works of F. Rabelais. Done out of French by Sir Tho. Urchard, Kt. and others. For R. Baldwin. 5v. (Wing R104, R109 (v.2). —Volume 3 is dated 1693; v.4-5 have title: Pantagruel's voyage to the oracle of the bottle . . . Done out of French by Mr. Motteux. [Wing R107].)

REYNARD THE FOX. The most delectable history of Reynard the Fox. T. James, for E. Brewster. (Wing S3513. Sixteenth edition.)

SCARRON, PAUL. Scarron's Novels. R. Everingham, for R. Bentley, W. Hinchman, F. Sanders, D. Browne, and J. Knapton. (Wing S835. Fourth edition.)

SCARRON INCENSED. Scarron incens'd, or His appearing to Madame Maintenon, his late wife: reproaching her amours with Lewis the Great. Written by a lady in French. R. Taylor. (Wing S838)

SERGEANT, JOHN. An historical romance of the wars, between . . . Gallieno, and . . . Nasonius. Doublin: Printed. (Wing S2570)

THREE CHOICE NOVELS. Three novels. The husband forc'd to be jealous [by Desjardins]. The drudge [by René le Pays]. The Cimmerian matron [by W. Charleton]. J. Langley. (Private library. —Made up of sheets of original editions, 1668, 1673, 1668, with general title-page canceling title-page of first tale.)

UNHAPPY LOVERS. The unhappy lovers: or, The timorous fair one. A novel. For R. Bentley. (Wing U67)

VALENTINE AND ORSON. Valentine and Orson, the two sons of the Emperour of Greece. J. W. for E. Tracy. (Wing V33. Fourteenth edition.)

1695

AULNOY, MARIE CATHERINE HORTENSE DE BERNEVILLE, comtesse d'. Memoirs on [sic] the Court of England, written by way of letters, by the Countess of Dauncy. For S. Darker. (Advertised in Athenian Mercury, June 23, 1695.)

BLIND BEGGAR. The history of the blind beggar of Bednal-green. For J. Blare. [ca.1695?] (Esdaile. Fourth edition.)

BUNYAN, JOHN. The pilgrim's progress. The fourteenth edition. For W. P. (Wing B5575. Nineteenth edition. —New York Public Library has two editions with this imprint and date; one has Bunyan on its title-page, the other has Bvnyan. Twentieth edition.)

BUNYAN, JOHN. The pilgrim's progress. The third part. The second

edition. By W. O. for J. Back and J. Blare. (Wing B5584. Second edition of this spurious continuation.)

CERVANTES SAAVEDRA, MIGUEL DE. The history of the ever-renowned knight Don Quixote de la Mancha. W. O., sold by H. Green. [1695?] (Wing C1773. First edition of this abridgment.)

CROUCH, NATHANIEL. The history of the nine worthies of the world. By R. B. For N. Crouch. (Wing C7338. Second edition.)

CROUCH, NATHANIEL. The unfortunate court favorites of England. By R. B. For N. Crouch. (Wing C7351)

ELIZABETH, Queen. The secret history of the most renown'd Q. Elizabeth, and the E. of Essex, by a person of quality. Cologne [London]: For Will with the wisp [i.e. R. Bentley]. [1695?] (Wing S2345. Fifth edition.)

FORDE, EMANUEL. The famous history of Montelion. For W. Thackeray, and E. Tracey. (Wing F1531. Eleventh edition.)

GUY OF WARWICK. The renowned history, or The life and death of Guy Earl of Warwick. A. M. for P. Brooksby. (Esdaile. Third edition of this version; preface signed John Shurley.)

JOHNSON, RICHARD. The pleasant delightful history of Tom of Lincoln. [J. Blare?] [ca.1695?] (Esdaile. —An abridgment.)

MACHIAVELLI, NICCOLO. The marriage of Belphegor. (In: The works of the famous Nicholas Machiavel. For R. Clavel, C. Harper, J. Amery, J. Robinson, A. and J. Churchil, sold by C. Harper, and A. and J. Churchil. Wing M131. Seventh edition.)

OLIVER OF CASTILE. The history of Olivaires of Castile, and Arthur of Dalgarve. From the Italian made English [by Mark Micklethwait, M. A.]. For F. Hildyard. (Wing H2129)

PLEASURES OF MATRIMONY. The pleasures of matrimony, intermix'd with variety of merry and delightful stories. For H. Rhodes. (Wing P2566. Fifth edition.)

ROUSSEAU DE LA VALLETTE, MICHEL. The life of Count Ulfield. Done out of French. Printed, 1695. (Wing R2052)

VANEL, CHARLES. The royal mistresses of France; or, The secret history of the amours of all the French kings. For H. Rhodes, and J. Harris. 2 pts. (Wing V90)

1696

AESOP. Æsop's Fables in prose and verse, the second part. By R. B. For N. Crouch. (Esdaile. —Cf. Crouch's *Delightful fables*, 1691. —The 35th of 40 editions of the fables in English during the period down to 1700.)

AESOP. Aesops Fables, with their morals. The thirteenth edition. For R. Bentley, J. Phillips, H. Rhodes, and J. Taylor. (Esdaile. Unidentified edition, of which first edition apparently appeared in 1650; the 36th of 40 editions of the fables in English during the period down to 1700.)

ALCANDER AND PHILOCRATES. Alcander and Philocrates: or, The pleasures and disquietudes of marriage. A novel. Written by a young lady. For R. Parker, S. Briscoe, and S. Burrowes. (University of Illinois Library)

AYRES, PHILIP. The revengeful mistress . . . also three other novels. For

R. Wellington. (E s d a i l e. —Some copies have variant imprint: For R. Bentley, and R. Wellington. [Wing A4313].)

BEHN, APHRA. The deceived lovers . . . V. The courtezan deceived. An addition to The lucky mistake. (Esdaile, without imprint.)

BEHN, APHRA. The histories and novels. For S. Briscoe. (Wing B1711. First edition.)

BEHN, APHRA. The histories and novels. For R. Wellington. (Esdaile. Second edition.)

BUNYAN, JOHN. The holy war. Assigns of B. A., sold by N. Ponder. (Wing B5540. Third edition.)

BUNYAN, JOHN. The life and death of Mr. Badman. The third edition. For W. P., sold by N. Ponder. (Wing B5553. Fourth edition.)

BUNYAN, JOHN. The pilgrim's progress. The second part. The seventh edition. For W. P. (Wing B5582. Seventh edition.)

CONSTANTINI, ANGELO. A pleasant and comical history of the life of Scaramouche. Translated by A. R. from the French copy. For R. Gifford. (Wing C6950)

COURTLZ DE SANDRAS, GATIEN. The memoirs of the Count de Rochefort. F. L. for J. Knapton, R. Parker, and T. Nott. (Wing C6600. First edition.)

COURTILZ DE SANDRAS, GATIEN. The memoirs of the Count de Rochefort. The second edition. For J. Sturton and A. Bosvile. (Wing C6600A. Second edition.)

DELONEY, THOMAS. The pleasant and princely history of the gentle craft. W. Wilde, sold by P. Brooksby, J. Deacon, J. Back, J. Blare, and E. Tracy. (Wing D962. Nineteenth edition.)

FAUST. The history of the damnable life and deserved death of Dr. John Faustus. W. O. for J. Back. [1696?] (Wing H2155. Twelfth edition.)

FAUST. The history of the wicked life and miserable end of Dr. John Faustus. W. O. for J. Back. [1696?] (Esdaile. —An abridgment.)

FORDE, EMANUEL. The most famous, delectable, and pleasant history of Parismus. The fourteenth impression. W. Wilde, sold by the booksellers. 2v. (Wing F1539, F1540. Eighteenth edition.)

GESTA ROMANORUM. A record of ancient histories, entituled in Latin: Gesta Romanorum. Glasgow: R. Sanders. (Wing R639. Twenty-second edition.)

GREENE, ROBERT. The pleasant and delightful history of Dorastus . . . and Fawnia. For G. Conyers. [1696?] (Wing G1832. Twentieth edition. —Appended at end is *The history of Josephus the Indian prince*.)

JOHNSON, RICHARD. The famous history of the seven champions of Christendom. For R. Chiswell, M. Wotton, G. Conyers, and B. Walford. 3v. (Wing J800, J803, J804. Fifteenth edition. —Volume 2 has imprint: W. Onley, for R. Chiswell [etc.]; v.3, For J. Back.)

LE NOBLE, EUSTACHE, sieur de Tennelière. Abra-Mulè, or A true history of the dethronement of Mahomet IV. Made English by J. P. For R. Clavel. (Wing L1051)

MANDEVILLE, Sir JOHN. The voyages & travels of Sir John Mandevile, knight. For R. Chiswell, B. Walford,

M. Wotton, and G. Conyers. (Wing M417. Eighteenth edition.)

MANLEY, MARY DE LA RIVIERE. Letters written by Mrs. Manley. To which is added A letter from a supposed nun in Portugal, to a gentleman in France . . . by Colonel Pack. For R. B. (Wing M434)

PALAIS ROYAL. The Palais Royal, or The amours of the French king and Madam Lavalier. Translated out of French, by T. B. For R. Bentley. (British Museum. Second edition.)

PIX, MARY. The inhumane cardinal, or innocence betray'd. A novel. Written by a gentlewoman. For J. Harding and R. Wilkin. (Newberry Library. —Dedication signed Mary Pix.)

QUEVEDO Y VILLEGAS, FRANCICO DE. Visions. Made English by Sir Roger L'Estrange. The eighth edition. For R. Sare and E. Hindmarsh. (Wing Q202. Tenth edition.)

VALENTINE AND ORSON. Valentine and Orson, the two sons of the Emperour of Greece. J. W. for E. Tracy. (Cited by Esdaile, with question mark, from the Term Catalogues. Fifteenth edition.)

1697

ART OF CUCKOLDOM. The art of cuckoldom: or, The intrigues of the city-wives. Sold by the booksellers. (Wing A3790)

AULNOY, MARIE CATHERINE JUMELLE DE BERNEVILLE, comtesse d'. The ingenious and diverting letters of the Lady ————. The fourth edition. For S. Crouch. (Wing B2039. Fourth edition; no third edition known.)

AULNOY, MARIE CATHERINE JU-
MELLE DE BERNEVILLE, com-
tesse d'. Memoirs of the court of
France. For E. Whitlock (Wing
A4219. Second edition.)

BARLAAM AND JOASAPH. The
history of the five wise philosophers.
By H. P. The second edition. For E.
Tracy. (Esdaile. Second edition.)

BERN, APHRA. The histories and
novels. The third edition. For R.
Wellington. (Esdaile. Third edition.)

BUNYAN, J O H N. The pilgrim's
progress. The third part. The third
edition. For J. Back. (Esdaile.
Third edition.)

FEMALE FALSEHOOD. Female falshood: or, The unfortunate beau.
Written by Monsieur S. Evremont.
And now made English. E. Whitlock.
(Wing S303. —A translation of *Memoires de la vie du comte D****, commonly attributed to Pierre de Villiers
and sometimes incorrectly to St.
Evrémond. —A second part was entered in the Term Catalogues for
1705.)

FORDE, EMANUEL. The famous
history of Montelion. The fourth edition. (Cited by Esdaile, without imprint, from the Term Catalogues.
Twelfth edition.)

FOUR NOVELS. Four novels in one
vol. Viz. The gallants, or, The reciprocal confidents. In two parts. The
amours of the Sultana of Barbary.
The amours of Philantus and Bellamond. For F. Saunders. (Wing
F1663)

HEAD, R I C H A R D. The English
rogue. The four parts. To which is
added a fifth part. The fourth edition. For J. Back. (Esdaile. Fourth
edition.)

HEAD, RICHARD. The life and
death of Mother Shipton. W. Onley
for J. Back. (Wing H1261. Sixth
edition.)

QUEVEDO Y VILLEGAS, FRANCI-
CO DE. Fortune in her wits, or,
The hour of all men. Translated into
English by Capt. John Stevens. For
R. Sare, F. Saunders, and T. Bennet.
(Wing Q188)

REYNARD THE FOX. The most
pleasing and delightful history of
Reynard the Fox, and Reynardine his
son. In two parts. W. Onley, sold by
H. Nelme. (Chapin Library. Second
edition of this abridgment.)

SEVEN SAGES. The history of the
seven wise masters of Rome. J. W.
for G. Conyers. (Wing H2187. Fourteenth edition.)

1698

AESOP. Aesops Fables, with the morals. The fourteenth edition. For J.
Phillips, H. Rhodes, and J. Taylor.
(Wing A708. Unidentified version;
the 37th of 40 editions of the fables
in English during the period down
to 1700.)

BEHN, APHRA. All the histories and
novels. The third edition. For S.
Briscoe. (Wing B1712. A re-issue of
the third edition?)

BEHN, APHRA. The unfortunate
bride: or, The blind lady a beauty.
For S. Briscoe. (Wing B1772. First
edition.)

BEHN, A P H R A. The wandering
beauty. S. Briscoe. (Wing B1773B)

GESTA ROMANORUM. A record of
ancient histories entituled in Latin:
Gesta Romanorum. For T. Basset, R.
Chiswell, A. Mill, G. Conyers, and M.

Wotton. (Wing R640. Twenty-third edition.)

GESTA ROMANORUM. The young man's guide to a vertuous life. In many pleasant little tales or allegories.. For G. and M. Conyers. (Wing Y118. —An abridgment.)

LA CALPRENEDE, GAUTIER DE COSTES, sieur de. Hymen's Praeludia; or, Love's master-piece. For R. Smith. (Newberry Library. A re-issue of the 1687 edition.)

LOVE IN DISTRESS. Love in distress; or, The lucky discovery, a novel. Written by the IIon. Lady ***. (Advertised for H. Newman in 1698.)

1699

AESOP. The Fables of Aesop and other eminent mythologists. By Sir Roger L'Estrange, Kt. The third edition. For R. Sare, B. Took, M. Gillyflower, A. & J. Churchil, G. Sawbridge, and H. Hindmarsh. 2v. (Wing A709. Third edition of this version; the 38th of 40 editions of the fables in English during the period down to 1700. —Volume 2 has title: *Fables and storyes moralized. Being a second part* . . . For R. Sare, 1699.)

AULNOY, MARIE CATHERINE JUMELLE DE BERNEVILLE, comtesse d'. Memoirs of the Countess of Dunois . . . written by her self before her retirement. For T. Cockerill. (Wing A4218. —Translated by J. H.)

AULNOY, MARIE CATHERINE JUMELLE DE BERNEVILLE, comtesse d'. Tales of the fairys. Translated from the French. For T. Cockerill. (Esdaile)

BEHN, APHRA. The histories and novels. For R. Wellington, sold by R. Tuckyr. (Wing B1713. Fourth edition?)

BIDPAI. The fables of Pilpay. For D. Brown, C. Connigsby, D. Midwinter and T. Leigh. (Wing B2885. First edition of this version.)

BREMOND, GABRIEL DE. The happy slave, a novel. Translated from the French. By a person of quality. The third edition. For R. Wellington, and E. Rumbal. (In: *A Collection of novels*, 1699. —See below. Fourth edition.)

BREMOND, GABRIEL DE. The viceroy of Catalonia: or, The double cuckold. Made English by James Morgan, Gent. For R. Wellington: and E. Rumball. (In: *A Collection of novels*, 1699. —See below. Second edition.)

CERVANTES SAAVEDRA, MIGUEL DE. The much-esteemed history of the ever-famous knight, Don Quixote de la Mancha. For N. Boddington. (Wing C1778. —Second edition of the 1689 abridgment apparently.)

COVENT GARDEN. The adventures of Covent Garden, in imitation of Scarron's City romance. H. Hills for R. Standfast. (Wing A604)

CROUCH, NATHANIEL. Unparallel'd varieties. The third edition. For N. Crouch. (Wing C7354. Third edition.)

CROUCH, NATHANIEL. Wonderful prodigies of judgment and mercy. By R. B. The fifth edition. For N. Crouch. (Wing C7362. Fifth edition; no fourth edition known.)

DEFOE, DANIEL. The compleat mendicant: or, Unhappy beggar. Being the life of an unfortunate gentleman. For E. Harris. (Wing D830. First edition.)

ELIZABETH, Queen. The secret history of the most renowned Q. Clizabeth [sic], and the Earl of Essex. By a person of quality. For R. Wellington: and E. Rumball. 2 pts. (In: *A Collection of novels,* 1699. —See below. Sixth edition.)

FENELON, FRANÇOIS DE SALIGNAC DE LA MOTHE. The adventures of Telemachus the son of Ulysses. Translated from the French [by Isaac Littlebury (and Abel Boyer?)]. For A. and J. Churchil. (Wing F674. First edition. —Incomplete; ends early in book 5.)

FORDE, EMANUEL. The famous and pleasant history of Parismus. In three parts. W. O., sold by J. Blare and G. Conyers. (Wing F1522. —An abridgment.)

NOVELS. A collection of novels. For R. Wellington and E. Rumball. (Wing C5149. —Contains: The secret history of the Earl of Essex and Queen Elizabeth. —The happy slave. —The victory of Catalonia. —The art of pleasing in conversation. —A second volume appeared in 1700.)

REYNARD THE FOX. The most delectable history of Reynard the Fox. [Parts 1 and 2.] For E. Brewster. (Esdaile. Seventeenth edition.)

WINSTANLEY, WILLIAM. The Essex champion: or The famous history of Sir Billy of Billerecay. For J. Blare. (Wing W3059A. Second edition.)

WOMAN'S MALICE. Woman's malice, a novel; being the true history of the amours of an eminent person of quality. For J. Wilde. (Wing W3324)

AESOP. Aesop's Fables, English and Latin. By Charles Hoole. R. E. for the Company of Stationers. (Wing A710. Second (or possibly first) appearance of this version; the 39th of 40 editions of the fables in English during the period down to 1700.)

AESOP. The fables of Aesop, with his life and fortune. [For G. Conyers?] (Esdaile. Caxton's version; the 40th of 40 editions of the fables in English during the period down to 1700.)

ALFRED. The history of the famous and renowned Alfred Prince of England. C. Brown and T. Norris. [ca. 1700] (C. A. Stonehill 149:160)

AMADIS DE GAULE. The history of Amadis de Gaul. For E. Tracy. (Esdaile. —An abridgment.)

AMADIS DE GAULE. The most excellent and famous history of the most renowned knight Amadis of Greece. B. Deacon. (Esdaile. Third edition.)

ARMSTRONG, JOHNNY. The pleasant and delightful history of the renowned northern worthy, Johnny Armstrong. W. O. [ca.1700] (Esdaile. —Wing P2531 lists an edition printed for T. Norris, sold by S. Bates, but the date given, [169-?], is probably too early.)

BARLAAM AND JOASAPH. The history of the five wise philosophers. By H. P. The second edition. For E. Tracy. (Wing P947. Third edition.)

BARNWELL, GEORGE. The prentice's tragedy: or, The history of George Barnwell. W. O. [ca.1700] (Esdaile)

BATEMAN'S TRAGEDY. Bateman's tragedy; or, The perjur'd bride justly rewarded. C. Brown, and T. Norris. [ca.1700] (Folger Library)

BEHN, APHRA. All the histories and novels. For R. Wellington, sold by R. Tuckyr. (Wing B1714. Fifth edition?)

BEHN, APHRA. Histories, novels, and translations. The second volume. W. O., for S. B., sold by M. Brown. (Library of Congress. First appearance of this volume.)

BEHN, APHRA. The unfortunate bride. For S. B. (Wing B1773. Second edition.)

BEVIS OF HAMPTON. The gallant history of the life and death of that most noble kmight [sic] Sir Bevis of Southampton. A. M. for B. Deacon. [ca.1700] (Wing G171 (?, which gives J. Deacon). Second edition of this version.)

BREMOND, GABRIEL DE. The pilgrim. Translated into English by P. Belon, Gent. For R. Wellington: and E. Rumball. 2v. (In: *A collection of pleasant modern novels*, 1700. —The second volume is Bellon's continuation of the story. Third edition.)

BUNYAN, JOHN. The holy war. For A. and J. Churchill. (Esdaile. Fourth edition.)

BUNYAN, JOHN. The life and death of Mr. Badman. For A. and J. Churchil. (Esdaile. Fifth edition.)

BUNYAN, JOHN. The pilgrim's progress. The third part. The fourth edition. W. Onley for J. Back. (Wing B5585. Fourth edition of this spurious continuation.)

C., L. Youth's pleasant recreation, or Merry pastime. Containing delightful sotries and novels. For T. Ballard. (Term Catalogues, III, 187)

CASTILLO SOLORZANO, ALONSO DEL. The life of Donna Rosina, a novel. Done into English, by the ingenious Mr. E[dward] W[ood]. B. Harris. [1700?] (Wing C1232. —An abridgment of his *La picara*.)

CAWWOOD. The pleasant history of Cawwood the Rook. W. O. [ca.1700] (Esdaile. Fifth edition.)

CERVANTES SAAVEDRA, MIGUEL DE. The history of the most ingenious knight, Don Quixote de la Mancha. Formerly made English by Thomas Shelton; now revis'd . . . by Captain John Stevens. For R. Chiswell, R. Battersby, A. and F. Churchill, S. Smith and B. Walford, M. Wotton, and G. Conyers. 2v. (Wing C1773A. First edition of this translation.)

CERVANTES SAAVEDRA, MIGUEL DE. The history of the renown'd Don Quixote de la Mancha. Translated from the original by several hands: and publish'd by Peter Motteux. For S. Buckley. 2v. (Wing C1775. First edition of this translation. —The last 2v. of the 4v. set appeared in 1703.)

CHAMILLY, NOEL BOUTON, marquis de. Five love-letters written by a cavalier, in answer to the five love-letters written to him by a nun. For R. Wellington, and E. Rumbold. (Newberry Library. Third edition.)

CHEVY CHASE. The famous and renowned history of the memorable but unhappy hunting on Chevy-Chase. W. O. [ca.1700] (Wing F360. Second edition.)

CHRISTIAN PILGRIM. The progress of the Christian pilgrim. For the author. (Wing P3653)

CONGREVE, WILLIAM. Incognita: or, Love and duty reconcil'd. A novel. For R. Wellington. (Wing C5849. In: *A collection of pleasant modern novels*, 1700. Second edition.)

COURTILZ DE SANDRAS, GATIEN. The French spy: or The memoirs of Jean Baptiste de la Fontaine. For R. Basset. (Wing C6597A)

CRAWFORD, D. Several letters; containing the amours of I. The unfortunate dutchess. . . II. Love after enjoyment. . . III. The unhappy mistake. . . By Mr. D. Cr————rd, Gent. For J. Austin. (Colin Richardson, 87:112)

CYNTHIA. Cynthia; with the tragical account of the unfortunate loves of Almerin and Desdemona. (Esdaile, without imprint. Second edn.)

DALERAC, FRANÇOIS PAULIN. Polish manuscripts: or, The secret history of the reign of John Sobieski. For H. Rhodes, T. Bennet, A. Bell, T. Leigh, and D. Midwinter. (Wing D127)

DEFOE, DANIEL. The compleat mendicant: or, Unhappy beggar. For E. Harris. (Esdaile, with question mark. Second edition.)

DELONEY, THOMAS. The pleasant history of John Winchcomb in his younger years called Jack of New-bery. The fifteenth edition. For E. Tracy. [1700?] (Wing D965. Sixteenth edition.)

DIVERSIONS OF MARS AND VENUS. The diversions of Mars and Venus consisting of several love stories as told by little Cupid to . . . his mother. Bath: (Gay, III, 83)

EDWARD IV. The amours of Edward IV. An historical novel. By the author of The Turkish spy. For R. Sare.

(Wing M565. —Attribution to G. P. Marana usually rejected.)

ELIZABETH, Queen. The history of the most renowned Queen Elizabeth and her great favorite, the Earl of Essex. A romance. W. O. [1700?] (Esdaile. Seventh edition. —Wing H2173 has same title, but with imprint: W. O., sold by C. Bates; date given of [1700] probably too early.)

ELIZABETH, Queen. The secret history of the most renowned Q. Elizabeth and the E. of Essex. For Will with the wisp [i.e. R. Bentley]. (Esdaile. Eighth edition. —This undated edition arbitrarily dated by being placed here —Wing S2346 has same title, but with imprint For R. Wellington and E. Rumball, and is said to be in *A collection of pleasant novels*; perhaps same as that listed in 1699.)

FAUST. The history of the damnable life and deserved death of Dr. John Faustus. C. Brown for M. Hotham. [n.d.] (Wing H2156, with date [1700?]; a date of [ca.1705] probably better. Thirteenth edition.)

FENELON, FRANÇOIS DE SALIGNAC DE LA MOTHE. The adventures of Telemachus. The second edition. For A. and J. Churchil. (Wing F674A. Second edition.)

FENELON, FRANÇOIS DE SALIGNAC DE LA MOTHE. The adventures of Telemachus. The third edition. For A. and J. Churchil. (Harvard University Library. Third edition.)

FORDE, EMANUEL. The famous and pleasant history of Parismus. In two parts. W. Onley for J. Blare, and for G. Conyers. [1700?] (Wing F1545. —Another edition (or issue) of the 1699 abridgment.)

90

FORDE, EMANUEL. The famous and pleasant history of Parismus. W. Onley for J. Blare. [ca.1700] (Wing F1521. —Abridgment? Same as preceding?)

FORDE, EMANUEL. The famous, pleasant, and delightful history of Ornatus and Artesia. For B. Deacon. [ca.1700] (Wing F1531A. Third edition of this abridgment.)

FORTUNATUS. The comical and tragical history of Fortunatus. Abbreviated for the good and benefit of young men and women. For C. Brown. [ca.1700] (Folger Library)

FRIAR BACON. The famous history of Fryer Bacon. For W. Thackeray, and C. Bates. [ca.1700] (Esdaile. Tenth edition.)

FRIAR BACON. The history of Fryer Bacon: the second part. For J. Blare. [ca.1700] (Esdaile)

FRIAR BACON. The most famous history of the learned Fryer Bacon. [ca.1700,] (Wing M2887, without imprint)

GOLDEN EAGLE. The famous and delightful history of the Golden Eagle. W. O. [ca.1700] (Esdaile. Third edition.)

GREENE, ROBERT. The pleasant and delightful history of Dorastus and Fawnia. W. O. for G. Conyers. [ca.1700] (Folger Library. Twenty-first edition.)

GREENE, ROBERT. The history of Dorastus and Fawnia. For J. Blare. [ca.1700] (Folger Library. —An abridgment.)

GUY OF WARWICK. The famous history of Guy of Warwick. Written by Samuel Rowland [sic]. For G. Con-

yers. [ca.1700] (Esdaile. —Turned into prose from Rowlands' verse.)

HARRINGTON, JAMES. The Oceana . . . and his other works. The whole [edited] by John Toland. Sold by the booksellers. (Wing H816. Fourth edition.)

HEAD, RICHARD. The life and death of the English rogue. For E. Tracy. [ca.1700] (Wing H1263. Second edition of this abridgment of part 1.)

HEYWOOD, THOMAS. The famous and remarkable history of Sir Richard Whittington. Written by T. H. C. Brown, and T. Norris, for E. Tracy. [ca.1700] (Wing H1780A. Fourth edition.)

HOWARD, THOMAS. The history of the seven wise mistresses of Rome. W. O., for G. Conyers. [ca.1700] (Wing H3010. Fifth edition.)

HOWARD, THOMAS. Roman stories: or, The history of the seven wise mistresses of Rome. The twelfth edition. T. Sabine. [ca.1700] (Wing H3011A. Sixth edition?)

KEACH, BENJAMIN. The progress of sin; or The travels of Ungodliness. The third edition. For N. Boddington. (Wing K82. Third edition.)

KEACH, BENJAMIN. The travels of True Godliness. The fourth edition. I. Dawks for N. Boddington. (Wing K100. Seventh edition.)

LAUGH AND BE FAT. Laugh and be fat, or An antidote against melancholy. To which is added, nine delightful tales. For J. How. (Term Catalogues, III, 174)

MALORY, Sir THOMAS. Great Britain's glory: or, The history of the life and death of K. Arthur. [ca.1700] W. O. (Wing S64. Second edition.)

MALORY, Sir THOMAS. Great Britain's glory: or, The history of the life and death of K. Arthur. [ca.1700] C. Brown. (Wing S65. Third edition.)

NOVELS. A collection of pleasant modern novels. Vol. II. Viz. Heroine musqueteer: or female warrier, in ofur [sic] parts. Incognito: or Love and duty reconciled. The pilgrim, in two parts. For J. Tonson, and R. Wellington: E. Rumbole, and J. Wild. (Folger Library. —Volume 1 appeared in 1699 under slightly different title.)

PALLADINE. The excellent history of Paladine of England. The second edition. J. F., sold by J. Marshall. [1700?] (Wing C5090A. Fourth edition. —The British Museum Catalogue also lists a re-issue of this with different title-page and imprint: Printed and sold by the booksellers. [1700?])

PRECHAC, JEAN DE. The heroine musqueteer: or, The female warriour. A true history. Translated out of French. J. Orme, for R. Wellington. (In: *A collection of pleasant modern novels,* 1700. Second edition. Wing P3207.)

REYNARD THE FOX. The history of Reynard the Fox, and Reynardine his son. In two parts. For the booksellers. [ca.1700] (Wing H2137. An abridgment. —Preface signed D. P.)

ROBIN HOOD. The noble birth and gallant atchievements of . . . Robin Hood. For B. Deacon. (Esdaile, with question mark, from Deacon's advertisement. Fifth edition.)

SCARRON, PAUL. Scarron's Novels. Fourth edition. For R. B. and R. W., sold by J. Wild. (Wing S836. Fifth edition. —Translated by John Davies.)

SCARRON, PAUL. The whole comical works. Translated by Mr. Tho. Brown, Mr. Savage. And others. For S. and J. Sprint, J. Nicholson, R. Parker, and B. Tooke. (Wing S829)

SAINT EVREMOND, CHARLES MARGUETEL DE SAINT DENIS, seigneur de. The works. In II. volumes. For A. and J. Churchill. (Wing S301. —Volume 1 contains a version of the Ephesian matron, pp. 236-241; volume 2 contains "A Novel [The Irish prophet]", pp. 78-99.)

SEVEN SAGES. The history of the seven wise masters of Rome. For J. Deacon. (Esdaile. Fifteenth edition.)

SHIRLEY, JOHN. The famous history of Aurelius, the valiant London-prentice. For B. Deacon. (Esdaile. Fourth edition.)

SHIRLEY, JOHN. London's glory: or, The history of the famous and valiant London prentice. W. O., sold by E. Tracy. [ca.1700?] (Esdaile. Some as above? Fifth edition?)

SIDNEY, Sir PHILIP. The most pleasant and delightful history of Argalus and Parthenia. W. O. for E. Tracy. [ca.1700] (Esdaile. Fifth edition.)

VAIRASSE, DENIS. The history of the Sevarites or Sevarambi. For W. Whitwood. 2v. (Wing V20B. Second edition.)

VALENTINE AND ORSON. Valentine and Orson, the two sons of the Emperour of Greece. A. M. for E. Tracy. [1700] (Wing V32 and P3363. Sixteenth edition.)

INDEX

Abu Bakr ibn al-Tufail, Abu Jafar, An account of the Oriental philosophy: 1674.
    History of Hai Eb'n Yockdan: 1686.
Achilles Tatius, Clitophon and Leucippe: 1638.
Adamite: 1683.
Adelaide: 1686.
Adolphus, The history of: 1691.
Aeneas Sylvius. See: Pius II.
Aesop, Fables (Ayres' version) : 1689.
            (Brinsley's version) : 1617, 1624.
            (Caxton's version) : 1611, n.d., 1628, 1634, 1647, 1685, 1676, 1700.
            (Crouch's version) : 1696.
            (Hoole's version) : 1689, 1700.
            (L'Estrange's version) : 1692, 1694, 1699.
            (Peacham's version) : 1646.
            (Philipott's version) : 1666, [1666?].
            (Sturtevant's version) : 1602.
            (Unidentified versions) : 1650, 1651, 1657, 1670, 1691, 1696, 1698.
Albions Queen, The famous history of: 1600, 1601.
Alcander. See: Courtilz de Sandras, Gatien.
Alcander and Philocrates: 1696.
Alcoforado, Marianna d', Five love-letters: 1678, 1680, 1686, 1693.
                  Seven Portuguese letters: 1681, 1693.
                  See also: Chamilly, Noel Bouton, marquis de.
Aleman, Mateo, Guzman de Alfarache: [1661?]
    The rogue: 1622, 1623, 1630, 1634, 1655, 1656.
Alfred, History of the famous: [1700?]
Aloisia. See: Blessebois, P. C.
Altophel and Astrea: 1678.
Amadis de Gaule: 1618, 1619, 1652.
    (abridgment) : 1685, [1700]
    Fifth book: 1664.
Amadis of Greece: 1693, 1694, 1700.
Amorous abbess: 1684.
Amorous convert: 1679.
Amorous travellers: 1671.
Amours of Madame. See: Henrietta.
Amours of the French court. See: French court.
Annals of love: 1672.
Anne, of Austria, Amours of: 1689, 1691.
Anton, Robert, Moriomachia: 1613.
Antonius and Aurelia: 1682.
Appollonius of Tyre: 1607.
Apuleius, Golden ass: 1639.
Argences,   d', Countess of Salisbury: 1683, 1692.

93

Armin, Robert, Foole upon foole: 1600, 1605.
       A nest of ninnies: 1608.
Armstrong, Johnny: [1700]
Art of cuckoldom: 1697.
Assarino, Luca, La Stratonica: 1651.
Audiguier, Henri Vital d', Lisander and Calista: 1621, 1627, 1635, 1652.
       Love and valour: 1638.
Aulnoy, Marie, comtesse d', Ingenious letters: 1691, 1692, 1697.
       Memoirs of the Countess de Dunois: 1699.
       Memoirs of the court of England: 1695.
       Memoirs of the court of France: 1692, 1697.
       Memoirs of the court of Spain: 1692.
       Novels of Elizabeth: 1680-81.
       Present court of Spain: 1693.
       Tales of the fairys: 1699.
Ayres, Philip, Revengeful mistress: 1696.

B., A. The mad men of Gotham: 1613, 1619, 1630, 1690.
Baarlam and Joasaph, Five wise philosophers: 1672, 1697, 1700.
Bacon, Sir Francis, New Atlantis: 1626, 1627, 1628, 1631, 1635, 1639, 1651, 1658,
       1659, 1660, 1664, 1670, 1676, 1677, 1683, 1685.
Balbulo and Rosina. See: Bear.
Baldwin, William, Beware the cat: 1652.
Barclay, John, Argenis: 1625, 1628, 1629, 1636, 1640.
Barnes, Joshua, Gerania: 1675.
Baron, Robert, An apologie for Paris: 1649.
       Erotopaigeion: 1647, 1648.
Barrin, Jean, Venus in the cloyster: 1683.
Barnwell, George, The prentice's tragedy: 1700.
Bateman's tragedy: 1700.
Bayly, Thomas, Herba parietis: 1650.
       The wall flower: 1679.
Bear, Beware the beare: 1650.
Behn, Aphra, Adventures of the black lady: 1684.
       Amours of Philander and Sylvia: 1687.
       Deceived lovers: 1696.
       Fair jilt: 1688.
       Histories and novels: 1696, 1697, 1698, 1699, 1700.
       History of the nun: 1689.
       Love-letters: 1683, 1684, 1693, 1694.
       Lucky mistake: 1689.
       Oroonoko: 1688.
       Three histories: 1688, 1689.
       Unfortunate bride: 1698, 1700.
       Wandering beauty: 1698.
    See also: Villains.
Beling, Richard, Sixth book to the Arcadia: 1624.
Belleforest, François de, Hystorie of Hamblet: 1608.

Bellianis, The honour of chivalrie: 1650, 1663, 1671, 1673, 1678, 1683.
        Honour of chivalry, part 2: 1664, 1671, 1673.
        Honour of chivalry, part 3: 1672, 1673.
Bellon, Peter, Amours of Bonne Sforza: 1684.
        Court secret: 1689.
        Reviv'd fugitive: 1690.
        Pilgrim. See: Bremond, Gabriel de.
        Princess of Fess. See: Prechac, Jean de.
Beraldus, prince of Savoy: 1675.
Bernard, Catherine, Count of Amboise: 1689.
        Female prince: 1682.
Bernard, Richard, The isle of man: 1626, 1627 bis, 1628, 1630, 1632, 1634, 1635,
        1640, 1648, 1658, 1659, 1668, 1674, 1676, 1677, 1683.
Bettie, W., Titana and Theseus: 1608, 1636.
Bevis of Hampton: 1689, 1691, 1700.
Bidpai, Fables of Pilpay: 1699.
        Moral philosophy of Doni: 1601.
Biondi, Giovanni F., Coralbo: 1655.
        Donzella desterrada: 1635, 1663.
        Eromena: 1632.
        Love and revenge: 1690.
Black Tom, The unlucky citizen: 1686.
Blackbourn, Richard, Clitie: 1688.
        Three novels in one: 1688.
Blair, Bryce, Vision of T. Verax: 1671.
Blessebois, P. C., Aloisia, or, The amours of Octavia: 1681.
Blind beggar of Bednal-green: 1676, 1686, 1695.
Blondo, Giuseppe, Penitent bandito: 1663.
Boccaccio, Giovannni, Decameron: 1620, 1625, 1634, 1655, 1657.
        Novels: 1684.
Boisrobert, François le Metel de, Annaxander and Orazia: 1639, 1657.
Bonnecorse, Balthazar de, Art of making love: 1688.
        La montre: 1686.
Borde, Andrew. See: B., A.; Scoggin.
Boursault, Edme, Deceptio visus: 1671.
        Prince of Conde: 1675.
Bovinian, The most pleasant history of: 1656.
Boyle, Robert, Martyrdom of Theodora and of Didymus: 1687.
Boyle, Roger, Earl of Orrery, English adventures: 1676.
        Parthenissa: 1651, 1654, 1655, 1656, 1669, 1676.
Brathwait, Richard, Arcadian princess: 1635.
        Ar't asleep hubsand: 1640.
        History of moderation: 1669.
        Panthalia: 1659.
        The penitent pilgrim: 1641.
        Two Lancashire lovers: 1640.
Bremond, Gabriel de, Cheating gallant: 1677.
        Gallant memoirs: 1681.

Happy slave: 1677, 1678, 1685, 1699.
Hattige: 1676, 1680, 1683.
Pilgrim: 1680-81, 1684, 1700.
Princess of Montferrat: 1680-81.
Triumph of love over fortune: 1678.
Viceroy of Catalonia: 1678, 1699.
See also: Colonna, Hortense (Mancini).
Breton, Nicholas, Grimellos fortunes: 1604.
Miseries of Mavillia: 1606.
Two excellent princes: 1600.
Brewer, Thomas, Merry devil of Edmonton: 1631.
Brillac, J. B. de, Agnes de Castro: 1688.
Brinsley, John. See: Aesop.
Brusoni, Girolamo, Arnaldo: 1660.
Bulteel, John, Birinthea: 1664.
Burton, John, Eriander: 1661.
Bunyan, John, The holy war: 1682, 1684, 1696, 1700.
Mr. Badman: 1680, 1685, 1688, 1696, 1700.
Pilgrim's progress: 1678, 1679, 1680, 1681, 1682, 1683, 1684, 1685, 1688, 1689, 1693, 1695.
Pilgrim's progress, part 2: 1684, 1686, 1687, 1690, 1693, 1696.
Pilgrim's progress, part 3: 1693, 1695, 1697, 1700.

C., A. See: Peppa.
C., H. See: Cox, H.
C., L., Youth's pleasant recreation: 1700.
C., N., A Saxon historie: 1634.
C., R. See: Codrington, Robert.
C, S., Cleocreton and Cloryana: [1630?], 1661.
C., T. See: Fortunatus, A right [etc.]; G., J.
C., W., Fragosa King of Aragon: 1618, 1646, 1656, 1663, 1664.
Cabinet opened: 1690.
Cacoethes leaden legacy: [1634].
Camus, Jean Pierre, Admirable events: 1639.
Diotrephe: 1641.
Elsie: 1655.
Forced marriage: 1678.
The loving enemie: 1650, 1667.
Natures paradox: 1652.
True tragical history: 1677, 1678.
Capello and Bianca: 1677.
Carleton, Rowland, Diana Dutchess of Mantua: 1679, 1681 (as Italian princess).
Carmeni, Francesco, Nissena: 1652, 1653.
Cartigny, Jean de, Voyage of the wandering knight: 1607, [1609?], [1626?], 1650, 1661, 1670, 1687 (as The conviction of worldly-vanity).
Castillo Solórzano, Alonso de, La picara: 1665.
Donna Rosina: [1700?].
Castro, Don Henriquez de: [1686].

96

Cavendish, Margaret, Duchess of Newcastle, Description of a new world: 1666, 1668.
    Natures pictures: 1656, 1671, 1674.
Cawwood the rook: 1640, 1656, 1683, [1700].
Ceriziers, Rene de, Innocency acknowledg'd: 1645.
    The innocent lady: 1654, 1674.
    The innocent lord: 1655.
    The triumphant lady: 1656.
Cervantes Saavedra, Miguel de, Delight in severall shapes: 1654.
    Don Quixote: (Shelton's tr.) : 1612, 1620, 1652, 1672-75.
              (Phillips' tr.) : 1687.
              (Motteux' tr.) : 1700.
              (Stevens' tr.) : 1700.
              (abridgements) : 1686, 1688, 1689, 1695, 1699.
    Exemplarie novels: 1640.
    Jealous gentleman of Estremadure: 1681.
    Persiles and Sigismunda: 1619.
    Select novels: 1694.
    Troublesome adventures. See: Codrington, R.
Cespedes y Meneses, Gonzalo de, Auristella: 1683.
    Gerardo: 1622, 1653.
Chamberlayne, William, Eromena: 1683.
Chambers, Robert, Palestina: 1600.
Chamilly, Noel Bouton, marquis de, Five love-letters: 1683, 1694, 1700.
Character of love: 1686, 1692.
Charles, Duke of Mantua. See: Leti, Gregorio.
Charleton, Walter, The Cimmerian matron: 1684.
    The Ephesian matron: 1659.
    The Ephesian and Cimmerian matrons: 1651, 1668. (Also in Three choice novels, 1694.)
Chaucer, Junior, pseud. Canterbury tales: 1687.
Chaucer's ghoast. See: Ovid.
Chavigny de la Bretonniere, François de, Gallant Hermaphrodite: 1687, 1688.
    Inconstant-lover: 1671.
Chevalier Del, pseud. See: Chamilly, Noel Bouton.
Chevreaux, Urbain. See: La Roche Guilhem, Mlle. de.
Chevy-chase, Famous history of: 1690, 1700 bis.
Children in the wood, History of: 1687.
Choice novels and amorous tales: 1652.
Christian pilgrim: 1700.
Churchyard, Thomas. See: Fortunatus, A right [etc.].
Circle, The. See: Montfort, François.
Claude, Isaac, Count d'Soissons: 1688.
Cleocreton and Cloryana. See: C., S.
Clerio and Lozia: 1652, 1655.
Cloria, The princess Cloria: 1661, 1665.
Cloria and Narcissus: 1653, 1654.
Cobbler of Canterbury: 1608, 1614, 1630, 1681.
Cobbler turned courtier. See: Henry VIII.

Codrington, Robert, The troublesome and hard adventures in love: 1652.
Coleraine, Hugh Hare, Situation of Paradise found out; 1683.
Collection of novels. See: Novels.
Colonna, Hortense (Mancini), The apology: 1679.
Congreve, William, Incognita: 1692, 1700.
Constantini, Angelo, Scaramouche: 1696.
Conquest of France. See: Edward the Black Prince.
Conversations at the grate. See: Adamite.
Corrozet, Gilles, Memorable conceits: 1602.
Cotton, Charles. See: Fair one of Tunis; Ovid.
Courtilz de Sandras, Gatien, Amorous conquest of Alcander: 1685.
      French spy: 1700.
      The history of . . . that gallant Captain Viscount de Turenne: 1686.
      Memoirs of Count de Rochefort: 1696.
Covent Garden, Adventures of: 1699.
Coveras, Francisco de las. See: Quintana, Francesco de.
Cox, H., Travels of love and jealousy: 1693, 1690 (as Lisarda).
Crafty lady: 1683.
Crawford, D., Several letters: 1700.
Crispe, Samuel, Don Samuel Crispe: 1660.
Croke, Charles, Fortune's uncertainty: 1667.
Crouch, Humphrey, Hodg of the south: 1655.
Crouch, Nathaniel, Delightful fables: 1691.
      Extraordinary adventures: 1683, 1685.
      Female excellency: 1688.
      History of the nine worthies: 1687, 1695.
      Surprizing miracles: 1683, 1685.
      Unfortunate court favorites: 1695.
      Unparallel'd varieties: 1683, 1685, 1699.
      Wonderful prodigies: 1681, 1682, 1685, 1699.
Crowne, John, Pandion and Amphigenia: 1665.
Cynthia: 1687, 1700.
Cyrano de Bergerac, Hercule Savinien de, Comical history: 1687.
      Selenarchia: 1659.

Dalerac, François Paulin, Polish manuscripts: 1700.
Dancer, John. See: Dauncey, John.
Dangerfield, Thomas, Dangerfield's memoirs: 1685.
      Don Tomazo: 1680.
Daniel, Gabriel, Voyage to the world of Cartesius; 1692, 1694.
Dauncey, John, English lovers: 1661-62.
Deceptio visus. See: Boursault, Edme.
Defoe, Daniel, Compleat mendicant: 1699, 1700.
Dekker, Thomas, A knights conjuring: 1607.
      Newes from Hell: 1606.
      The wonderful year: 1603 bis, 1604.
Dekker and Wilkins, Jests: 1607.
Delightful novels: 1685 bis, 1686 bis.

Deloney, Thomas, Gentle craft: 1627, 1635, 1637, 1639, 1640, 1648, 1652, 1660,
[1670], 1672, 1674, [1675], 1676, 1678, 1685, [1690], 1696.
Jack of Newbery: 1619, 1626, 1630, 1633, 1637, 1655, 1672, [1690], [1700].
abridgment: 1684.
Thomas of Reading: 1612, 1623, 1632, 1636, 1672, 1690.
abridgment: 1690.
Democrates: 1679.
Desjardins, Marie Catherine, Amours of the Count de Dunois: 1675.
Disorders of love: 1677.
Husband forc'd to be jealous: 1668. (Also in Three choice novels, 1694.)
Love's journal: 1671.
Loves of sundry philosophers: 1673.
Memoirs of Henrietta Moliere: 1672-77.
Unfortunate heroes: 1679.
Desmarets de St. Sorlin, Jean, Ariana: 1636, 1641.
Disorders of Basset. See: Prechac, Jean de.
Diversions of Mars and Venus: 1700.
Dobson, George, Dobsons dry bobs: 1607.
Don Juan Lamberto. See: Montelion, pseud.
Don Tomazo. See: Dangerfield, Thomas.
Doni, Antonio. See: Bidpai.
Du Bail, Louis Moreau, sieur, Famous Chinois: 1669.
Dunton, John: Hue and cry after conscience: 1685.
Informer's doom: 1683.
Pilgrim's guide: [1684].
Voyage round the world: 1691.
Du Prat, Abbe, pseud. See: Barrin, Jean.
Dutch rogue: 1683.
Dutch whore. See Trumbull.
Du Vignan, Turkish secretary: 1688.

Edward IV, Amours of: 1700.
Edward, the Black Prince, Conquest of France: [1680].
Eliana: 1661.
Elizabeth, History of . . . and Earl of Essex: [1700].
Secret history of Duke of Alencon and: 1691.
Secret history of . . . and E. of Essex: 1680, 1681, 1689, 1695, 1699, 1700.
English monsieur: 1679.
English princess. See: Prechac, Jean de.
Erastus. See: Seven sages.
Erotopolis: 1684.
Essex champion. See: Winstanley, William.
Estienne, Henri, A world of wonders: 1607, 1608.
Evagoras. See: L., L.
Eve revived: 1684.
Evordanus: 1605.
Extravagant poet. See: Oudin, Cesar F.

Fair one of Tunis: 1674.
Fatal prudence. See: Democrates.
Fauconbridge: 1616, 1635.
Faust: 1608, 1618, 1622, 1636, 1648, 1674, 1677, 1682, [1687], 1690, 1696, [1700]
    abridgment: [1685], [1690], [1696].
Faust, Second report of: [1674], 1680, 1685, [1687].
Female falshood: 1697.
Fenelon, François de Salignac, Adventures of Telemachus: 1699, 1700.
Fernandez, Girolamo. See: Bellianis.
Fidge, George, The English Gusman: 1652.
        Hind's ramble: 1651.
        Wit for money: 1652.
Fieux, Charles de. See: French rogue.
Firedrake, Sir, The knight-adventurer: 1663.
Five love-letters. See Alcoforado, Marianna d'; Chamilly, Noel Bouton.
Five wise philosophers. See: Barlaam and Joasaph.
Flores, Don. See: Herberay, Nicolas de.
Flores, Juan de, Aurelio and Isabell: 1608.
        A pair of turtle doves: 1606.
Floridon and Lucina. See: P., J.
Foigny, Gabriel de, New discovery of Terra incognita: 1693.
Fontaines, Louis, Relation of Jansenia: 1668.
Force of love. See: Triumph of friendship.
Forde, Emanuel, Montelyon: 1633, 1640, 1661, 1663, 1668, 1671, 1673, 1677, 1680,
        1687, 1695, 1697.
        Ornatus and Artesia: 1607, 1619, 1634, 1650, 1662, 1669, 1683.
            abridgment: [1688], [1694], [1700].
        Parismus: 1608-09, 1615, 1630, 1636, 1649, 1657, 1660, 1661, 1663, 1664,
            1665, 1668, 1669, 1671, 1672, 1677, 1681, 1684, 1689, 1696.
            abridgment: 1677, 1683, 1699, [1700].
Fortunate lovers: 1632, 1683. See also: Three excellent new novels.
Fortunatus, The right, pleasant, and variable history: 1676, 1679, 1682, [1689].
        The history of the birth of: 1650, 1682.
        abridgments: [1685], [1700].
Four novels in one volume: 1697.
Fragosa, King of Aragon. See: C., W.
Frank, John, Birth, life and death of: [1690].
French court, History of the amours of: 1684.
French rogue: 1672, 1694.
Friar Bacon, Famous history of: 1627, 1629, 1640, 1661, 1666, 1679, 1682, 1683,
        [1700].
        Second part of: [1700].
        Most famous history of (abridgment?): [1700].
Friar Rush. See: Rush, Friar.
Frith, John, Witty jests: 1673.
Frolicksome, Sir Humphrey, The merry Oxford knight: 1650.
Frost, An historical account of: 1684.
Fugitive statesman: 1683.
Fuller, Thomas. See: Triana.

Furetiere, Antoine, Scarron's City romance: 1671.

G., D.   See: Sunday's adventures.
G., J., City revels: [1690].
G., R.   See: Albions Queen.
Gainsford, Thomas, Trebizond: 1616.
Gallants, The.   See: Poisson, Raymond.
Gallant ladies, The.   See: Poisson, Raymond.
Gallantry unmasked: 1690.
Garcia, Carlos, Guzman, Hinde, and Hannam outstript: 1657.
   Lavernae: 1650.
   Son of the rogue: 1638.
George a Greene: 1632.
George, Saint, Life and death of: 1660, [1675].
German princess revived: 1684.
Germont, de, The Neapolitan: 1683.
Gesta Romanorum: 1660, 1602, 1610, [1610?], [1620?], [1639], 1648, 1650, 1662,
   1663, 1668, 1672 bis, 1681, 1682, 1689, 1696, 1698 bis.
Gibbs, Richard, New disorders of love: 1687.
Gildon, Charles, Post-boy rob'd of his mail: 1692-93.
Glanville, Joseph, Essays: 1676.
Godwin, Francis, The man in the moon: 1638, 1657.
Godwin, Paul, Histoire des larrons: 1638.
Golden Eagle, History of the: 1672, 1677, [1700].
Gombauld, Jean Ogier de, Endymion: 1639.
Gomberville, Marin Le Roy, sieur de, Polexander: 1647, 1648.
Goodman, Nicholas, Hollands Leaguer: 1632.
Goulart, Simon, Admirable and memorable histories: 1607.
Governor of Cyprus.   See: Virotto and Dorothea.
Gracián Dantisco, Lucas, Galateo espagnol: 1640.
Gracian y Morales, Baltasar, The critick: 1681.
Graham, Richard.   See: Preston, Richard Graham, viscount.
Greene, Robert, Alcida: 1617.
   Arbasto: 1617, 1626.
   Card of fancy: 1608.
   Ciceronis amor: 1601, 1605, 1609, 1611, 1616, 1628, 1639.
   Dorastus and Fawnia: 1648, 1655, 1664, 1675, 1677, 1684, 1688, [1690],
    1694, [1696], [1700]
     abridgments: [1690], [1700]
   Euphues his censure: 1634.
   Farewell to folly: 1617.
   Groatsworth of wit: 1600, 1616, 1617, 1621, 1629, 1637.
   Mourning garment: 1616.
   Menaphon: 1605, 1610, 1616, 1634.
   Never too late: 1600, 1602, 1607, 1611, 1616, [1620?], [1630?], 1631.
   Pandosto: 1607, 1609, 1614, 1619, 1629, 1632, 1636.
   Penelopes web: 1601.
   Philomela: 1615, 1631.
Grenadine, Sebastian, Homais Queen of Tunis: 1681.

Grimalkin, or The rebel-cat: 1681.
Griselda, Antient, true and admirable history of: 1607, 1619.
Griselda, Pleasant and sweet history of: [1640], 1686.
    True and admirable history of: 1663, 1674 bis, 1682.
Guillet de St. George, Georges, Voyage to Athens: 1676.
Guy of Warwick (Rowlands' version): [1700].
    (Shirley's version): 1681, 1685, 1695.
    (Smithson's version): [1661], 1686.

H., T. See: Heywood, Thomas.
Hainam, Richard. See: S., E.
Hall, Joseph, Discovery of a new world: [1609?], [1613?].
    Psittacorum regio: 1669.
    Travels of Quevedo: 1684.
Hamblet. See: Belleforest, François de.
Harrington, James, Oceana: 1656, 1658, 1700.
Hart, Alexander, Alexto and Angelica: 1640.
    See also: Hipolito.
Head, Richard, English rogue: 1665, 1666, 1667, 1668, 1671, 1674, 1680, 1688, 1689,
        1693, 1697, 1700.
    abridgments: 1679, 1688.
    Complaisant companion: 1674, (Later eds. as Nugae venales.)
    Floating island: 1673.
    Life and death of Mother Shipton: 1667, 1677, 1684, 1687, 1694, 1697.
    Miss displayed: 1675, 1683.
    News from the stars: 1673.
    Nugae venales: 1675, 1686, 1687.
    Western wonder: 1674.
Heliodorus, An Aethiopian history: 1605, 1606, 1622, 1627, 1686, 1687 (as
        Triumphs of love and constancy).
Helvetian hero, Adventures of the: 1694.
Henrietta, Princess, The amours of Madame: 1680.
Henry VIII, Cobler turned courtier: 1680.
    Pleasant history . . . and a cobler: [1690].
    Pleasant history of . . . and Abbot of Reading: [1690].
Herberay, Nicolas de, Most excellent history of Don Flores: 1664, 1677.
Hero and Leander, Famous and renowned history of: [1690].
Heywood, Thomas, Famous history of Whittington: 1656, 1678, 1680, [1700].
Hickathrift, Thomas, Pleasant history of: [1675]
Hind, James, No jest like a true jest: [1670], 1674, 1680, [1690?].
    The pleasant history of: 1651.
Hind, John, Eliosto libidinoso: 1606.
    Lysimachus and Varrona: 1604.
Hipolito and Isabella: 1628, 1633.
Histoire des larrons: 1638.
Holland, Samuel, Don Zara del Fogo: 1656.
    Romancio-mastrix: 1660.
    Wit and fancy in a maze: 1656.
Honour of chivalry. See: Bellianis.

Howard, Thomas, Seven wise mistresses of Rome: 1663, 1684, 1686, 1688, [1700].
    Roman stories: [1700].
Howell, James, Dendrologia: 1640, 1644, 1645, 1649, 1650.
Huon of Bordeaux: 1601.
Husband forced to be jealous. See: Desjardins, Marie Catherine.
Hynd, John. See: Hind, John.
Hystorie of Hamblet. See: Belleforest, François de.

I., R., Tom Thumb: 1621.
Illustrious lovers. See: Prechac, Jean de.
Ingelo, Nathaniel, Bentivolio and Urania: 1660, 1664, 1669, 1673, 1682.
Intrigues of love: 1682, 1689.
Irish prophet. See: Saint Evremond, Charles.
Irish rogue: [1690].

Jack of Dover: 1604, 1608, 1615.
Johnson, John, The academy of love: 1641.
Johnson, Richard, Old Hobson: 1607, 1610, 1634, 1640.
    The seven champions of Christendom: 1608, [1612], 1623, [1626], [1639?],
        1660, 1670, 1675, 1676, 1680, 1686, 1687, 1696. (part 3: 1686, 1689,
        1694)
        abridgements: 1661, 1675, 1679.
    Tom a Lincoln: 1631, 1635, 1655, 1668, 1682.
        abridgement: [1695].

Keach, Benjamin, Progress of sin: 1684, 1685, 1700.
    Travels of True Godliness: 1683, 1684 ter, 1700.
Kepple, Joseph, Maiden-head lost by moon-light: 1672.
Kirkman, Francis, Unlucky citizen: 1673.
    See also: Clerio and Lozia; Head, Richard, English rogue; Bellianis,
        Bellianis, pt. 2.
Kittowe, Robert, Loves load-star: 1600.
Knight-adventurer. See: Firedrake, Sir.

L., L., Evagoras: 1677.
La Calprenède, Gautier de Costes, sieur de, Cassandra: 1652, 1661, 1664, 1667, 1676.
    Cleopatra, 1652.
    Hymen's praeludia: 1652, 1654, 1655, 1656, 1657, 1658, 1659, 1663, 1665,
        1668, 1674, 1687, 1698.
    Pharamond: 1662, 1677.
La Chappelle, Jean de, Unequal match: 1681-83.
Ladle, Tom, Pleasant hitsory of: [1690].
La Fayette, Marie Madeleine de, Princess of Cleves: 1679, 1688.
    Princess of Montpensier: 1666.
    Zayde: 1678, 1690.
La Ferte Senneterre, La Mareschalesse de, History of: 1690.
La Mothe, Marie Catherine. See: Aulnoy, Marie Catherine, comtesse d'.
La Roberdière, sieur de, Love victorious: 1684.

La Roche Guilhem, Mlle de, Almanzor and Almanzaida: 1678.
   Asteria and Tamberlain: 1677, 1690 (as Royal lovers).
   Great Scanderberg: 1690.
   Zingis: 1692.
Las Coveras, Francisco de. See: Quintana, Francesco de.
Laugh and be fat: 1700.
Lazarillo de Tormes: 1624, 1639, 1653, 1655, 1669-70, 1672-77, 1688, 1693.
Lebechea, D. de. See: Dutch rogue.
Lefevre, Raoul, Destruction of Troy: 1607, 1617, 1636, 1663, 1670, 1676, 1680, 1684.
Le Noble, Eustache, Abra-Mule: 1696.
   Amours of Ann. See: Anne, of Austria.
Le Pays, René, The drudge: 1673. (Also in Three choice novels, 1694.)
Leti, Gregorio, Charles, Duke of Mantua: 1669, 1685.
   See also: Messalina.
Le Vayer de Boutigny, Rolland, Tarsis and Zelie: 1685.
Lisander: 1681.
Lodge, Thomas, Rosalynde: 1604 bis, 1609, 1612, 1614, 1623, 1634, 1642.
London bully: 1683.
Long Meg. See: Meg.
Longus, Daphnis and Chloe: 1657.
Loredano, Giovanni F., Dianea: 1654.
   The life of Adam: 1659.
   Novells: 1682.
Love after enjoyment. See: Crawford, D.
Love in distress: 1698.
Love letters between Polydorus . . . . See: Messalina.
Love's empire: 1682.
Love's posie: 1686.
Lucian, Dialogues and true history: 1634.
   Part of Lucian made English: 1663, 1664.
   Works: 1684-85.
Luna, Juan de, Pursuit of Lazarillo: 1622, 1631, 1639.
Lyly, John, Euphues, pt. 1: 1605, 1606, 1607, 1613.
   Euphues, pt. 2: 1601, 1605, 1606, 1609.
   Euphues, both parts: 1617, 1623, 1630, 1631, 1636.

M., P., The Cimmerian matron. See: Charleton, Walter.
M., T., Nim: 1657.
Machiavelli, Niccolo, The divell a married man: 1647.
   Marriage of Belphegor: 1671, 1675 bis, 1680, 1694, 1695.
Mackenzie, Sir George, Aretina: 1660, 1661.
Madmen of Gotham. See: B., A.
Mainwaringe, M., Vienna: 1620, 1621, [1628?], [1632?], 1650.
Malory, Sir Thomas, Brittains glory: 1684.
   Great Britain's glory: [1700] bis.
   Morte Darthur: 1634.
Mandeville, Sir John, Voyages and travels: 1612, 1618, 1625, 1632, [1640?], 1650,
   1657, 1670, 1677, 1684, 1696.

Manley, Mary de la Riviere, Letters: 1696.
Marana, G. P.   See: Edward IV.
Marguerite de Navarre, Heptameron: 1654.
Marianus: 1641.
Markham, Gervase, The English Arcadia: 1607, 1613.
Matthew, Sir Tobie.   See: Blondo, Giuseppe.
May, Thomas.   See: M., T.
Mazarin, Hortense (Mancini), Memoires: 1676 bis, 1690, 1695.
Meg of Westminster: 1620, 1635, 1636.
Meroveus: 1682.
Merry companion: 1686.
Mervine: 1612.
Meslier.   See: Hipolito.
Messalina, Amours of: 1689.
        Love letters between Polydorus and: 1689.
        Royal wanton: 1689, 1690.
Money, Mrs., Death and burial of: 1664, 1678.
Montalvan, Juan Perez de.   See: Perez de Montalvan, Juan.
Montelion, pseud., Don Juan Lamberto: 1661 ter, 1664, 1665, 1677.
Montfaucon de Villars, Count of Gabalis: 1680 bis.
Montfort, François Salvat, sieur de, The circle: 1675, 1676.
        The politick and heroick vertues of love: 1686.
Montreux, Nicolas de, Honours academie: 1610.
More, Sir Thomas, Utopia: 1606, 1624, 1639, 1684, 1685.
Morgan, Sheffrey ap, Life and death of: [1690].
Morgan, Schon ap, Wonderful adventures of: [1690].
Morindos: 1609.

Neapolitan.   See: Germont,   de.
Neville, Henry, Isle of pines: 1688.
Newcastle, Margaret Cavendish, duchess of.   See: Cavendish, Margaret.
Nicerotis, History of: 1685.
Nicostratus: 1680.
Noel, Nathaniel.   See: Montfort, François.
North, Sir Thomas.   See: Bidpai.
Novels, Collection of: 1699-1700.

Obliging mistress: 1678.
Oceander: 1600.
Oldys, Alexander, Fair extravagant: 1682.
        Female gallant: 1692.
        London jilt: 1683, 1684.
Oliver of Castile: 1695.
Ortigue, Pierre d', sieur de Vaumoriere, Agiatis: 1686.
        The grand Scipio: 1660.
        Grand Scipio, v.2: 1661.
Ortuñez de Calahorra, Diego, Mirror of knighthood: 1601.
Ottoman gallantries: 1687.

Oudin, Cesar François, Extravagant poet: 1681.
Ovid, Chaucer's ghoast: 1672.

P., J., Floridon and Lucina: 1663.
P., J., Simon and Cisley: [1670].
Pagan prince: 1690.
Pair of turtle doves. See: Flores, Juan de.
Palais royal, The history of: 1680, 1696.
Palestina. See: Chambers, Robert.
Palladine, Famous history of: 1664, [1685], [1700] bis.
          abridgment: [1685].
Palmendos, Famous history of: 1653, 1663.
Palmerin d'Oliva: 1615, 1616, 1637.
Palmerin of England: 1602, 1609, 1616, 1639, 1664.
          abridgment: 1685, 1691.
Pamphilus, Hesychius, pseud. See: Brathwait, Richard.
Panton, Edward, Speculum juventutis: 1671.
Paris and Vienna. See: Mainwaringe, M.
Pasquils jests: 1604, 1609, 1629, [1632?], 1635.
Pasquin risen from the dead: 1674.
Pastime royal: 1682.
Patient Griselda. See: Griselda.
Patrick, Saint, Delightful history of: 1685.
Patrick, Simon, Parable of the pilgrim: 1665, 1667, 1668, 1670, 1673, 1678, 1687.
Peachum, Henry. See: Barlaam and Joasaph.
Peebles, The three priests of: 1603.
Peele, George, Merry conceited jests: 1607, [1620?], 1627 bis, 1657, 1671.
Penitent bandito. See: Blondo, Giuseppe.
Penitent hermit: 1679.
Penton, Stephen, Guardian's instruction: 1688.
          New instructions for the guardian: 1694.
Peppa: 1689.
Perez de Montalvan, Juan Aurora: 1647, 1650.
          The illustrious shepherdess: 1656.
Perplexed prince. See: S., T.
Perplexed princess. See: Zayas y Sotomayor, Maria de.
Petronius Arbiter, The satyr of: 1694.
Pettie, George, A petite pallace: 1608, 1613.
Philantus and Bellamond, Amours of: 1690, 1697.
Philaquila, pseud. See: Golden Eagle.
Phillips, William, A new faring: 1688.
Philoxypes and Polycrite: 1652.
Pierreville, Gideon. See: Religious cavalier.
Pius II (Aeneas Sylvius), Eurialus and Lucrecia: 1639.
Pix, Mary, Inhumane cardinal: 1696.
Player's tragedy: 1693.
Pleasant companion: 1684.
Pleasures of matrimony: 1688, 1689, 1693, 1695.

Plot in a dream: 1681.

Poisson, Raymond, Gallant ladies: 1685 bis (second time as The galants), 1697.

Pomerano, Castalio, pseud. See: Brathwait, Richard.

Poor Robin's visions: 1677.

Pope, Walter, Memoirs of Monsieur du Vall: 1670.

Portsmouth, Duchess of, Secret history of: 1690.

Practical part of love: 1660.

Prechac, Jean de, The amours of Count Teckeli: 1686.

       The chaste seraglian: 1685.

       Disorders of Basset: 1688.

       The English princess: 1678.

       The grand vizier: 1685 bis (second time as The true history of Cara Mustapha).

       The heroine musqueteer: 1678-79, 1700.

       The illustrious lovers: 1686.

       The illustrious Parisian maid: 1680.

       The lovely Polander: [1681]

       The princess of Fess: 1682.

       The serasquior bassa: 1685.

Preston, Richard Graham, viscount, Angliae speculum morale: 1670.

       Moral state of England: 1694.

Preti, Girolamo. See: Perez de Montalvan, Juan.

Price, Laurence, The witch of the woodlands: 1655, 1675, [1677], 1684.

       Witty William: 1674.

   See also: Valentine and Orson.

Primaleon of Greece: 1619.

Quevedo y Villegas, Francesco de, Buscon: 1657, 1670.

       Fortune in her wits: 1697.

       Hell reformed: 1641.

       Novels: 1671.

       Paul of Segovia. See: Cespedes y
         Meneses, Auristella.

       Town adventurer: 1675.

       Visions: 1640, 1667 bis, 1668 bis, 1671, 1673, 1675, 1678, 1682, 1689, 1696.

Quintana, Francesco de, Don Fenise: 1651.

Rabelais, François, Works: 1653, 1664, 1693-94.

Religious cavalier: 1683.

Reynard the Fox: 1620, 1629, 1640, 1650, 1654, 1656, 1662, 1681, 1694, 1699.

       abridgment: 1685, [1690], 1697, [1700].

       Second part: 1672, 1681.

       Third part (Shifts of Reynardine): 1684.

Reynolds, John, Blood for blood: 1661.

       Delightful novels. See under title.

       The flower of fidelitie: 1650, 1654, 1655, 1660.

       Garden of love: 1692.

       Glory of God's revenge: 1685, 1686, 1687, 1688.

Triumphs of Gods revenge: 1621, 1622 bis, 1623, 1624, 1629, 1635, 1639, 1640, 1657, 1662, 1663, 1670, 1679, 1682.
Rich, Barnaby, Rich his farewell: 1606.
Rival mother: 1692.
Rival princesses: 1689.
Rivers, George, The heroinae: 1639.
Roberts, Henry, Haigh for Devonshire: 1600, 1612.
      Pheander: 1617, 1661.
Robin Goodfellow: 1628, 1639.
Robin Hood, Noble birth of: 1662, 1678, 1685, [1690], [1700].
Robinson, R.   See: Gesta Romanorum.
Rosamond, Life and death of: [1670], [1680].
Rousseau de la Vallette, Michel, Casimir: 1681.
      Life of Count Ulfeld: 1695.
Royal wanton.   See: Messalina.
Rush, Friar: 1620, 1626, 1629, 1659.

S., E., The witty rogue: 1656.
S., J., Clidamas: 1639.
S., J.   See: Cartigny, 1687.
S., N., Merry jests: 1617.
S., T., Lysander and Sabina: 1688.
S., T., Perplexed prince: [1682].
S., T., Second part of the pilgrim's progress: 1682, 1683, 1684 bis.
Sack-full of newes: 1673.
Sadeur, Jacques, pseud.   See: Foigny, Gabriel de.
Saint Evremond, Charles, Works: 1700.
    See also: Female falsehood.
Saint Real, Cesar Vichard de, Don Carlos: 1674, 1676.
    See also: Mazarin, Hortense (Mancini) .
Salas Barbadillo, Alonso, The fortunate fool: 1670.
Salton, W., Somnia allegorica: 1661.
San Pedro, Diego de, Arnalt and Lucenda: 1608.
Saulnier, Gilbert, Sieur du Verdier, Love and armes: 1640, [1663].
Saxon history.   See: C., N.
Scarron, Paul, Comical romance: 1665, 1676.
      Novels: 1665, 1667, 1683, 1694, 1700.
      Unexpected choice: 1670.
      Whole comical works: 1700.
    See also: Furetiere, Antoine.
Scarron incens'd: 1694.
Schooten, Hendrik van, The hairy giants: 1671.
Scoggin, John, Scoggins jests: 1613, 1626, [1690].
Scudéry, Madeleine de, Almahide: 1677.
      Amaryllis to Tityrus: 1681.
      Artamenes: 1653, 1654, 1655, 1691.
      Clelia: 1655, 1656, 1658, 1660, 1661, 1677-78.
      Ibrahim: 1652, 1674.
Sebastian, Don Sebastian, King of Portugal: 1683.

Secret letters of amour: 1692.
Segrais, Jean. See: La Fayette, Marie Madeleine.
Sergeant, John, Wars between Gallieno and Nasonius: 1694.
Seven sages, Erastus: 1684.
       History of Prince Erastus: 1674.
       History of the seven wise masters of Rome: 1602, 1633, 1653, 1671, 1673,
             1677, 1682, 1684, 1687, 1688, 1693, 1697, [1700].
       Wisdom's cabinet opened: [1675].
Seven wise mistresses of Rome. See: Howard, Thomas.
Sheppard, Samuel, Amandus and Sophronia: 1650.
Sherman, Thomas. See: S., T., Second part of the pilgrim's progress.
Shipton, Ursula, Strange and wonderful history of: 1686.
Shirley, John, Famous history of Aurelius: [1675], [1690], 1692, [1700].
Sidney, Sir Philip, Arcadia: 1605, 1613, 1621, 1622, 1623, 1627, 1629, 1633, 1638,
       1655, 1662, 1674.
       Argalus and Parthenia: 1672, 1683, 1691, 1692, [1700].
Siege of Mentz: 1692.
Silesio, Mariano, pseud. See: Brathwait, Richard, The Arcadian princess.
Simon and Cisley. See: P., J.
Sorel, Charles, Francion: 1655, 1661.
       The extravagant shepherd: 1653, 1654, 1657, 1660.
Spanish and French history: 1689.
Spanish decameron: 1687.
Stitch, Tom, Wanton Tom: 1685.
Stukeley, The famous history: 1638.
Sturtevant, Simon. See: Aesop.
Subligny, Adrien de, The mock-Clelia: 1678.
Sultana of Barbary, Amours of: 1689, 1697.
Summers, Will, Pleasant history of: 1637, 1676.
Sunday's adventure: 1683.

Tachmas: 1676.
Tallemant, Paul, Lycidus: 1688.
Tarlton, Richard, Jests: 1611, 1613, 1638.
       News out of Purgatory: 1630.
Taxila, See: W., D.
Theophania: 1655.
Three choice novels: 1694.
Three excellent new novels: 1683, 1685. See also: Fortunate lovers.
Tinker of Turvey. See: Cobbler of Canterbury, 1630.
Tom the shoemaker: 1674.
Tom Tram: [1684], [1690].
Travels of love and jealousy. See: C., H.
Triana: 1654, 1664.
Triumph of friendship: 1684.
Trumbill, Dutch whore: 1690.
Tudor, a prince of Wales: 1678.
Turkish secretary. See: Du Vignan.
Twine, Laurence, Pattern of painfull adventures: 1607.

Two new novels: 1688.

Unfortunate dutchess. See: Crawford, D.
Unhappy lovers: 1694.
Unhappy mistake. See: Crawford, D.
Unlucky citizen. See: Black Tom; Kirkman, Francis.
Unsatisfied lovers: 1683.
Urano: 1605.
Urfe, Honore d', Astrea: 1620, 1657, 1658.

Vairasse, Denis, History of Sevarites: 1675-79, 1700.
Valentine and Orson: 1637, 1649, [1664], 1671, 1675, 1677, 1680, 1682, 1685, 1688,
          1694, 1696, [1700].
     abridgment: 1673, 1683.
Vanel, Charles, Royal mistresses of France: 1695.
Vaumoriere, Pierre d'Ortigue, sieur de. See: Ortigue, Pierre de.
Vega Carpio, Lope de, Pilgrim of Casteele: 1621, 1623.
Venus in the cloyster. See: Barrin, Jean.
Victorious lovers: [1680].
Villains, Lives of sundry notorious villains: 1678.
Villiers, Claude, Gentleman apothecary: 1670, 1678.
Villiers, Pierre. See: Female falshood.
Virotto and Dorothea: 1689.
Virtue rewarded: 1693.
Voiture, Vincent, Alcidalis: 1678.
       Zelinda: 1676.
Voss, Jenny. See: German princess revived.

W., A. See: Weamys, Anne.
W. D., Taxila: 1692.
Wanton friar: 1689.
Weamys, Anne, Continuation of Arcadia: 1651, 1690.
Westward for smelts: 1620.
Whittington, Sir Richard. See: Heywood, Thomas.
Wilkins, George, Pericles: 1608.
Winstanley, William, Honour of the merchant-taylors: 1668.
       Honour of the taylors: 1687, 1689.
       Essex champion: [1690], 1699.
   See also: Poor Robin's visions.
Wisdom's cabinet opened. See: Seven sages.
Woman's malice: 1699.
Wright, Thomas, Glory of God's revenge. See: Reynolds, John.
Wroth, Lady Mary, Countess of Montgomeries Urania: 1621.

Yorkshire rogue: 1684.
Youngman's guide: 1698.
Youth's pleasant recreation. See: C., L.

Zacharie de Lisieux. See: Fontaines, Louis.
Zayas y Sotomayor, Maria de, Perplexed princess: 1683.
Zelinda. See: Voiture, Vincent.